SPEAK TO YOUR STORM

TRANSFORMING STORMS INTO TRIUMPHS

LAUDZ NICOLAS

Trilogy Christian Publishers
A Wholly Owned Subsidiary of Trinity Broadcasting Network
2442 Michelle Drive
Tustin, CA 92780

For information, address Trilogy Christian Publishing
Rights Department, 2442 Michelle Drive, Tustin, Ca 92780.
Trilogy Christian Publishing/TBN and colophon are trademarks of Trinity Broadcasting Network.
For information about special discounts for bulk purchases, please contact Trilogy Christian Publishing.

10 9 8 7 6 5 4 3 2 1
Library of Congress Cataloging-in-Publication Data is available.
ISBN 979-8-89041-720-6
ISBN 979-8-89041-721-3 (ebook)

DEDICATION

This book is dedicated first and foremost to my children, Naike, Jaffrey, Isaiah, Jovhan, and Abigail, who, despite all the storms that they have been through in life, came out strong, victorious, and ready to take on this journey called life with the help of our Almighty God. They supported me and did their best to understand me in every endeavor that I felt that I was called to accomplish. Thank you for our restored relationships. I see and hear you. I love you so very much, and I am so proud of each one of you. I also dedicate this book to all the *storm survivors*. I greatly appreciate you. I pray that you will never be deterred or distracted and that you will reach your God-given potential. I want to encourage you. Never give up. I believe wholeheartedly that God has so much more in store for you.

God bless you.

FOREWORD

We are living in the most turbulent and disturbing times of change in history. Everything is being shaken. Unless we stand on a solid foundation, we will be tossed by every wind and wave. That is why we must draw closer to God and strengthen our faith. We desperately need a spiritual awakening.

Speak to Your Storm is the perfect guide to help you reignite your faith and find the strength you need to navigate through these difficult times. Open your heart and mind to allow the stories and insights within these pages to ignite you! Knowing how to speak to your storm with authority and power is critical. If not, your storm will always have power over you.

The personal stories in this book are a testament to the fact that God is still in the miracle-working business. From the depths of despair, these stories will inspire you to believe that all things are possible with God. He is and will always be in control. The stories Laudz shares may be personal, but the takeaways are universal. Each chapter is loaded with spiritual truths that will help you reinvent your life and rekindle your faith.

Laudz Nicolas candidly shares her emotions, fears, anger, and disappointments in a way that will resonate with you. They remind me of my own struggles and the storms I had to face in my own journey.

As a healing and deliverance minister, Laudz didn't just decide to write this book. She spent a long time praying and seeking guidance from the Holy Spirit to write the right words that will move you in a special way. You will discover on your own once you start reading *Speak to Your Storm*.

Her deep faith in God shines through every page. She reminds us that in the darkest of moments, God is fighting our battles even while we are sleeping. We just need to surrender and trust Him.

Now more than ever, we need a book like *Speak to Your Storm*. The takeaways will help you weather any storm, big or small. Whether you are looking for inspiration to help you live your best life or how to handle life's challenges, this book has it all.

The apostle Paul said, "We are hard-pressed on every side, but not crushed; perplexed, but not in despair; persecuted, but not abandoned; struck down, but not destroyed" (2 Corinthians 4:8–9, NIV). May you take heart in the knowledge that no matter what you face in life, you are not alone. With Christ as your anchor, you can weather any storm and emerge stronger on the other side.

Enjoy reading *Speak to Your Storm*. Get some copies for friends and family members.

Keep pressing on!

—Rene Godefroy
Award-Winning Author of *Kick Your Excuses Goodbye*

ACKNOWLEDGMENTS

Writing a book was harder than I thought it would be, but it was such a rewarding feeling when completed. I want to acknowledge my husband, Elisee, who supported me throughout the process; my friend, Bettina Eugene, who constantly tried to encourage me to take the time to finish the book; Reverend Pamela Gillard, who told me to review one page at a time and lovingly gave me a deadline. To my friend, Rene Godefroy, thank you for telling me that I had a story to tell. I am grateful for the hours of coaching, encouraging, and assisting in the design. And finally, thank you to all those who created some of the storms that I had to go through in my life; you made me stronger. To my daughter, Deborah Abigail, you are my cause of joy. Thank you for your continuous love and encouragement.

TABLE OF CONTENTS

INTRODUCTION

Many years ago, I found myself going through storm after storm. Life was so difficult, and I thought that it would never end. Growing up in the Catholic faith, I recited many prayers but never really paid attention to the words that I was constantly repeating. Many times, I hit rock bottom, but always, something would get a hold of me and help me to overcome. I have been through so many betrayals, deceitful relationships, and the subject of gossip. I have to admit that finding myself in certain situations was due to the decisions I made without being well-equipped or inquisitive enough. I found out that God, through every situation, was there and had a plan and a divine purpose for my life. Every time I spoke to someone about a dreadful situation and how I was able to overcome it, the answer was always the same: you should write a book, and so many people will be encouraged by those experiences. Leave it to God to take your mess and turn it into a message. It might sound like a cliché, but my life is proof that God can turn your tests into a testimony to His glory. I have heard many people say, "Why would God choose you? Why you?" And my answer is always, "If not me, then who?" I have a vivid testimony of what God can do to lift His children. I have been through so much that I can empathize with those going through the storms of life that I have had the privilege to go through to get to where I am today.

Read on and be encouraged! God has the final say.

CHAPTER 1:

KNOW THY ENEMY

It was mid-morning on a weekday as I sat on my bed listening to this worship song by Don Moen. His words weaved through the entire house. I considered the passion that drives Christians to want to stand in awe of God and offer our worship to Him with our entire being.

A feeling of fear gripped me. My body seemed to get colder—a strange and piercing pain twisted through my lower abdomen. I shivered like a leaf. I started praying while still being aware of the song playing in the background. I cried out to God to stop this pain. The feeling intensified.

After a while, I could no longer deal with such intense pain; the agony became more than my ability to connect to God. I started screaming.

As I took my eyes off the cross and focused on my flesh and the physical pain, I gave up. I withdrew from the spiritual realm and allowed my flesh to take control. I enabled my natural man and the pain to bring me to a breaking point. I wish I could tell you that I miraculously regained strength, took control, and overcame it, but I did not. Once I stopped praying and focused entirely on the pain, it felt like some invisible being was piercing my body with something undetectable to me. I became angry. Have you ever been in so much pain that you felt like you were losing your mind, and the only way to deal with the intense feeling of pain was to start throwing things under your hand? I was getting there, and I know myself to be a very calm and collected person, not easily given to emotional outbursts. I could not hold myself up and tried to stand coupled, holding my lower abdomen and tears gushing out of my eyes. I had forgotten about praying as I overlooked the melody that I was listening to. The white walls in my bedroom felt like a prison. I was trapped in that moment. I wondered where God was and what He was doing. After intense agony and discomfort, as suddenly as the pain came, the pain went away. As I recovered control of myself and my body, I thought that an eternity had passed, but it had only lasted a few minutes. This experience left me angry, disappointed, and disillusioned.

After a while, sitting back on my bed, feeling weak to the core and uneasy, I began to reminisce about the incident, asking myself in disbelief, "What happened? What was that?"

As I meditated on the whole situation, I wondered if it was a test from God. Was it an attack from the devil? Or was my body trying to convey to me that something was wrong and needed attention?

As a healing and deliverance minister, my mind immediately started racing that this could only be an attack from a foul spirit, a devilish attack from the enemy.

The enemy had been angry about the multiple healings and deliverances through my ministry and had found a way to attack me physically and weaken me. What was the attack?

Unexpected crises are a part of life; they are like storms. As it is with predicaments, they cannot be escaped. Even if you find shelter in a storm, it is still there, pounding away. Consequently, we need to learn how to prepare and ride them out. As with any crises, we must learn to make provisions and withstand them by training and maturing from them.

One of the great illustrations of both crises and storms in the Bible is in the book of Acts. Apostle Paul is headed from one prison in Jerusalem to one in Rome to appeal to Caesar. Paul and two hundred seventy-five (275) of his companions were headed straight to the biggest storm and crisis in their lives. The storm lasted many days, and they lost all hope until Apostle Paul, through the visit of an angel, reassured them.

When you are going through a storm, when unexpected problems find you, tribulations no matter what they may be, loss of a job, divorce, failed relationships, loss of a home, death of a child, sickness, disease, infirmity, you need to ask yourself: "Is it a storm? If it is a storm, where has it come from, and why am I going through this?" Then, work it out in prayer, in meditation in the presence of the Lord, and analyze the situation. We are so busy with life dealings that we seldom take the time to sit down and examine a situation. We allow life to drive us instead of us driving it, controlling as our God intended for us to do.

From that incident, I can say that I have been through many other storms in my life, but I have learned to recognize and deal with life storms.

If you don't know that you are going through a storm, you will not know how to deal with the storm and what steps to take. If you are not willing to face it, you will not be able to fix it. You will find yourself crippled by your storm and defeated. This book will provide you with nuggets of information and spiritual and biblical tactics to prepare you, strengthen you, and grant you the victory that God has already won for you.

WHAT IS A STORM?

First, let's define a storm. What is a storm? A storm, according to the Merriam-Webster Dictionary, is "a serious disturbance of any element of nature, a disturbed or agitated state. *Storms* of emotion, sudden or violent commotion, a heavy discharge of objects (as missiles), a tumultuous outburst. A *storm* of protests, a sudden heavy influx or onset, a violent assault on a defended position, a sudden occurrence of something in large amounts and/or a situation in which many people are angry, upset, etc." A storm causes devastation: a storm can be the reason for people's displacement, a storm creates havoc in someone's life. The dictionary also defines the word storm as a "strong or violent outburst, as of emotion or excitement; *a storm of tears, a* violent disturbance or upheaval, as in political, social, or domestic affairs, *a* violent, sudden attack on a fortified place, and a sudden attack by means of force."

A storm is anything that causes distress, makes one feel depressed, causes disturbances to one's routine and everyday life, or anything that enables one to slack in one's daily activities and negatively changes one's outlook on life. A storm can last one hour, or it can last days or months. A storm can strengthen you or weaken you. A storm is an event, an occurrence that is forcing you to worry, to lose sleep, to be anxious, to be discouraged. Do you have an idea of what the definition of a storm is? A storm can be a bad marriage, a misbehaved child, a sickness, a financial crisis, debt, a divorce that you went through, bankruptcy, bill collectors at your door, or any addiction. A storm can also be fighting actual demonic entities, actual strongholds in your life. These attacks can leave you in shock, make you feel violated and devastated, take you off the ground, and sweep even the ground from under your feet. Are you beginning to understand what I am talking about when I say storm? I am talking about what we call spiritual storms. Some storms can keep you up at night staring at the ceiling, making you so weak and frightened that you are no longer able to feel or be happy, not even with yourself.

Many people have gone through storms and did not make it because either they lacked relevant information or they lacked biblical knowledge. The most important part is that this will not be your portion, for this book will equip you to go through life's storms and succeed in dealing with them.

First, ask yourself: "Where am I? Am I about to enter a storm? Going through a storm or coming out of a storm? Is it even a storm?" You need to recognize your storm. You need to ask yourself: "Where is that storm coming from? Who is ultimately responsible for my storm?" And you need to plan. You must make some decisions. More importantly, what you should be mindful of is that no matter where the storm originated from, it can never be permanent. We go through life storms. The Bible says in Psalm 30:5 (ESV), "Weeping may endure for a night, but joy comes in the morning." But what you do during the storm, your attitude, preparation, and planning as you enter a storm and during a storm, and how you handle the storm will impact the result. Remember, the results will cancel the insults. It is crucial what you produce during a storm. Is the storm a storm of correction? Is it a storm of destruction? Is it God, or is it the devil? Or is it you? Someone has said that at any specific moment of our lives, we are either entering a storm, going through a storm, or coming out of a storm. Life is a succession of storms. Your attitude is what will determine your altitude.

If you are not living right, if things in your life do not align with the Word of God, if your character does not line up with God's character, you may be going through a storm of correction. The Bible says in Hebrews 12:7 (ESV), "It is for discipline that you have to endure. God is treating you as sons. For what son is there whom his father does not discipline?" And again, consider this in the book of Proverbs 3:12 (ESV), "for the Lord reproves him whom he loves, as a father the son in whom he delights."

CONFESS SIN

Many times, we bring crises onto ourselves. We accomplish this by sinning deliberately or by just making bad decisions and listening to inadequate advice. Have you ever met some folks who have told you that they are engaged in spiritual warfare, fighting demonic spirits when, in fact, they are fighting the consequences of their own actions? Hence, we must assess our part and make the necessary corrections. Seek His forgiveness and the forgiveness of others if necessary. We must be humble enough to allow the Holy Spirit to live in us. We rise to this status by opening our mouths not for food but for confession, admitting our mistakes, and being willing to correct them.

We cannot always seek to blame others or make excuses. I wish I could blame so many people for the wrong decisions I made in my life and the dire consequences I have paid because of them. At the end of the day, I had to consider that it was my decision to do what I did, to choose the paths I chose, to even agree to what someone else has advised me to do. Even if I was blinded by my emotions, I was a willing participant, and I allowed bad things to happen to me. I used to hate speaking up and offending others. By my refusal to confront people for what they did or intended to do to me, I permitted resentment and bitterness to rent space in my heart. I agree, however, that people will betray you and try to ruin your life; even so, you have to take responsibility for allowing it to happen or look at your motives and behavior.

Being responsible may not be the politically correct thing to do, but it is what a godly disciple of Christ does. This is the mark of a genuine and emotionally mature Christian. Sacrificing to change can sometimes be inevitable and something that is good for you.

If you are going through a storm, you need to work this out in prayer and establish where you are and who is doing it. One hour in the presence of God will reveal any laid-out plan, whether for you or somebody else. When you get on your knees, the Holy Spirit will reveal to you the source of your storm. A storm of corrections can bring us to our lowest point and make us feel defeated. Even in a storm of correction, the enemy will step in and take advantage of the situation. If you know that you are going through a storm of corrections, allow the Lord to teach you the lesson and correct the behavior. Instead of crying out to God that you cannot sustain in this storm, tell your Father, who is teaching you, "Father, teach me. I am available." Kathryn Kuhlman, the great healing evangelist, once said that God is looking for available vessels. Tell God that you are available. Many times, we pray, asking God to take the storm away from us. What we should be praying to God is to give us the strength to go through the storm.

This is what will unlock your destiny. This is what will take us where God wants us to be; this is what will place us on the highway of our calling. This is what will make us discover our divine purpose. There are lessons to be learned, taught, and received. David went through storms as God dealt with him after he sinned, impregnated Bathsheba, and arranged to have Uriah killed to cover his indiscretion. Let's look at the scriptures in 2 Samuel 11:2–27:

> It happened, late one afternoon, when David arose from his couch and was walking on the roof of the king's house, that he saw from the roof a woman bathing; and the woman was very beautiful. And David sent and inquired about the woman. And one said, "Is not this Bathsheba, the daughter of Eliam, the wife of Uriah the Hittite?" So David sent messengers and took her, and she came to him, and he lay with her. (Now she had been purifying herself from her uncleanness.) Then she returned to her house. And the woman conceived, and she sent and told David, "I am pregnant."
>
> So David sent word to Joab, "Send me Uriah the Hittite." And Joab sent Uriah to David. When Uriah came to him, David asked how Joab was doing, how the people were doing, and how the war was going. Then David said to Uriah, "Go down to your house and wash your feet." And Uriah went out of the king's house, and there followed him a present from the king. But Uriah slept at the door

of the king's house with all the servants of his lord and did not go down to his house. When they told David, "Uriah did not go down to his house," David said to Uriah, "Have you not come from a journey? Why did you not go down to your house?" Uriah said to David, "The ark and Israel and Judah dwell in booths, and my lord Joab and the servants of my lord are camping in the open field. Shall I then go to my house, to eat and to drink and to lie with my wife? As you live, and as your soul lives, I will not do this thing." Then David said to Uriah, "Remain here today also, and tomorrow I will send you back." So, Uriah remained in Jerusalem that day and the next. And David invited him, and he ate in his presence and drank, so that he made him drunk. And in the evening, he went out to lie on his couch with the servants of his lord, but he did not go down to his house.

In the morning David wrote a letter to Joab and sent it by the hand of Uriah. In the letter he wrote, "Set Uriah in the forefront of the hardest fighting, and then draw back from him, that he may be struck down, and die." And as Joab was besieging the city, he assigned Uriah to the place where he knew there were valiant men. And the men of the city came out and fought with Joab, and some of the servants of David among the people fell. Uriah the Hittite also died. Then Joab sent and told David all the news about the fighting. And he instructed the messenger, "When you have finished telling all the news about the fighting to the king, then, if the king's anger rises, and if he says to you, 'Why did you go so near the city to fight? Did you not know that they would shoot from the wall? [21] Who killed Abimelech the son of Jerubbesheth? Did not a woman cast an upper millstone on him from the wall, so that he died at Thebez? Why did you go so near the wall?' then you shall say, 'Your servant Uriah the Hittite is dead also.'"

So the messenger went and came and told David all that Joab had sent him to tell. The messenger said to David, "The men gained an advantage over us and came out against us in the field, but we drove them back to the entrance of the gate. Then the archers shot at your servants from the wall. Some of the king's servants are dead, and your servant Uriah the Hittite is dead also." David said to the messenger, "Thus shall you say to Joab, 'Do not let this matter displease you, for the sword devours now one and now another. Strengthen your attack against the city and overthrow it.' And encourage him."

When the wife of Uriah heard that Uriah her husband was dead, she lamented over her husband. And when the mourning was over, David sent and brought her to his house, and she became his wife and bore him a son. But the thing that David had done displeased the LORD."

2 SAMUEL 11:2–27 (NRSV)

Do you remember that story in the Bible? It is a fact that David went through so many storms, but in it all, he gave himself to God and stayed at the feet of his Father. In God are our strength and our ability to resist and to bear.

In another narrative, God dealt with Saul when he met Jesus on the road to Damascus and was blinded for three (3) days. Apostle Paul knew well about storms. He dealt with physical and spiritual storms in his life because of the gospel of Jesus Christ. He says in the book of 2 Corinthians 11:23–27:

> Are they servants of Christ? I am a better one—I am talking like a madman—with far greater labors, far more imprisonments, with countless beatings, and often near death. Five times I received at the hands of the Jews the forty lashes less one. Three times I was beaten with rods. Once I was stoned. Three times I was shipwrecked; a night and a day I was adrift at sea; on frequent journeys, in danger from rivers, danger from robbers, danger from my own people, danger from Gentiles, danger in the city, danger in the wilderness, danger at sea, danger from false brothers; in toil and hardship, through many a sleepless night, in hunger and thirst, often without food, in cold and exposure.

2 CORINTHIANS 11:23–27 (ESV)

When Jesus was praying in the Garden of Gethsemane, He knew that something dreadful was coming, and He could only see victory manifested through the will of God. He prayed, "Nevertheless not my will but yours be done" (Luke 22:42, ESV). True victory resides in the will of God. Now, you ask me, "How do I distinguish that I am in a storm of correction?" In a storm of correction, the enemy will surely use all his tactics to confuse you. The answer lies in the presence of God. So many people spend their time in prayer speaking to the devil rather than to God, spending hours rebuking the devil, "Devil, I rebuke you, get away from me." Instead of speaking to God in their prayer time, they start speaking to the enemy. Our time in prayer is to be in the presence of the Almighty God, to replenish our souls, and to hear from our Father. Many people can't even pray; others, as soon as they start praying, the enemy starts speaking to their minds and distracting them. Listen, if you are not praying, you are playing. Let me tell you, I went through something similar. Every time I would decide to go into prayer, my mind would be racing with every thought; the enemy of my soul was playing his tricks on me. I could not concentrate, and I would become frustrated. I would not accomplish what I had set out to accomplish in the presence of God. I sought God, and in prayer, He responded. He revealed to me that the enemy was able to distract me and speak to me in my prayer time because my flesh was not crucified. I needed to stay in prayer long enough to bypass the fleshy stage, enter the spirit realm, and let the spirit realm control my flesh. Deep?

Today, many Christians cannot receive from God because they have not learned to go through the outer courts, enter behind the veil, and into the presence of God. Prayer is spending time with God. Prayer is taking your mind from your problems and concentrating on God. Prayer is giving praise to God. Prayer is interceding for others. Prayer is bringing your petitions and supplications to your father. Prayer is entering into the spirit realm, and suddenly, seeing tears coming out of your eyes and the Holy Spirit comforting you. Prayer is standing before the Throne of Grace, receiving mercy and grace as needed to strengthen you and help you to carry out your tasks. Some people spend more time speaking on the phone, texting, and Skyping than speaking to God. Prayer is committing your day, your family, and your whole being into the hands of your Father. How long do you stay in prayer? I have heard the term "microwave prayer" or "fast food prayer." Those are the prayers that last as long as it takes to microwave your food or the time it would take you to get your hamburger from a fast-food restaurant. If you want to touch the heart of God and be strengthened, you must stay in prayer. I pray for you today that God will put His fire on your prayer altar in Jesus's name. Say amen.

Let me further explain something to you. God purifies your spirit through wisdom and affliction as refiners purify metals in the furnace. "Afflictions?" you say. Oh yes. There is a verse in the Bible in the book of Isaiah 48:10 (ESV) that states, "Behold, I have refined you, but not as silver; I have tried you in the furnace of affliction." God will refine us like gold. Many references deal with the clay in the hands of the potter, which is also refined through fire. Our earthly being cannot change into gold. It must be melted and dissolved by means of the fire to separate every foreign particle. It needs to be cast again and again and again in the fire until there is nothing left to be purified and all traces of pollution have been disbanded. After this process is concluded, the gold can no longer be polluted. Any polluted item that brushes on gold that has been refined can only attach itself to the surface and cannot deeply affect it. It can only be short-term until the gold is wiped or swept and the polluted particle is erased. As sons of God, He refines us, prepares us, cleanses us, and develops us. This process that I am talking about can never be accomplished by us, the creatures. It is the work of our Creator. In the flesh, we resist what God wants to do with us. We fight the process we do not understand. I once heard the beautiful story of the teacup. I share it here with you. The author is unknown. Here is the story:

> There was a couple who used to go to England to shop in the beautiful stores. They both liked antiques and pottery, especially teacups. This was their twenty-fifth wedding anniversary. One day, in this beautiful shop, they saw a beautiful teacup. They said, "May we see that? We've never seen one quite so beautiful."
>
> As the lady handed it to them, suddenly, the teacup spoke. "You don't understand," it said. "I haven't always been a teacup. There was a time when I was red, and I was clay. My master took me and rolled me and patted me over and over, and I yelled out, 'Let me alone,' but he only smiled, 'Not yet.'"
>
> "Then I was placed on a spinning wheel," the teacup said, "and suddenly I was spun around and around and around. 'Stop it! I'm getting dizzy!' I screamed. But the master only nodded and said, 'Not yet.'"
>
> "Then he put me in the oven. I never felt such heat. I wondered why he wanted to burn me, and I yelled and knocked at the door. I could see him through the opening, and I could read his lips as he shook his head, 'Not yet.'"

"Finally, the door opened, he put me on the shelf, and I began to cool. 'There, that's better,' I said. And he brushed and painted me all over. The fumes were horrible. I thought I would gag. 'Stop it, stop it!' I cried. He only nodded, 'Not yet.'"

"Then suddenly, he put me back into the oven, not like the first one. This was twice as hot, and I knew I would suffocate. I begged. I pleaded. I screamed. I cried. All the time, I could see him through the opening nodding his head and saying, 'Not yet.'"

"Then, I knew there wasn't any hope. I would never make it. I was ready to give up. But the door opened, and he took me out and placed me on the shelf. One hour later, he handed me a mirror, and I couldn't believe it was me. 'It's beautiful. I'm beautiful.'"

"'I want you to remember, then,' he said, 'I know it hurts to be rolled and patted, but if I had left you alone, you would have dried up. I know it made you dizzy to spin around on the wheel, but if I had stopped, you would have crumbled. I knew it hurt and was hot and disagreeable in the oven, but if I hadn't put you there, you would have cracked. I know the fumes were bad when I brushed and painted you all over, but if I hadn't done that, you never would have hardened; you would not have had any color in your life. And if I hadn't put you back in that second oven, you wouldn't survive for very long because the hardness would not have held. Now, you are a finished product. You are what I had in mind when I first began with you.'"

When gold is first placed in the fire, it looks like it darkens first before brightening. Your soul, if it were to give consent to go through this process of decontamination, would surely cry, "No," but a soul that has given itself to Christ submits passively to his Maker for this process of purification. By this method, God purifies our souls. This process can last quite a long time, depending on the individual. I pray that you will not become dispirited by it but that you will yield yourself to the Holy Spirit until you are transfixed by the Spirit of God. Ask God for the strength to complete it. God knows what He's doing (for all of us). He is the Potter, and we are His clay. He will mold us and make us so that we may be made into flawless pieces of work to fulfill His good, pleasing, and perfect will. Jeremiah 18:6 (ESV) says, "O house of Israel, can I not do with you as this potter has done? declares the LORD. Behold, like the clay in the potter's hand, so are you in my hand, O house of Israel."

PREPARING FOR A STORM

I have to tell you that many times, we receive warning signs that a storm is on the way, but we fail to recognize them or we dismiss them. Where are you? If you are someone who uses discernment, you can often feel the wind of the storm blowing. You get a warning that a storm is coming, whether by revelation, a dream, a feeling, or some hints or incidents that precede the storm. Many of us, however, find ourselves unprepared and in unexpected storms. By the way, if you find yourself in the middle of a storm, don't panic. It happened to the disciples of Jesus; it happened to the best of us. But before I continue, I would like to share this with you. Those are things that you can watch out for. If you can detect the moment, you will be further along. If you can identify it, you will be able to rectify it. If you are willing to face it, you will be able to fix it. Some days, I will be working or accomplishing a regular task and suddenly feel uneasy, like tightness in my heart. That uneasy feeling would always cause me to start praying. At other times, I would be driving, and I would get that same uneasy feeling. Always, this would cause me to pray to God to exercise control over any attacks on me, my family, or any open doors that the enemy was trying to use at that moment. Many times, I have received a testimony from a friend or a family member, and they will say, "I got into a fight," or "Something was going wrong, and I felt that someone was praying for me." I will notice that the event had happened at the same time that I had that uneasy feeling that forced me to go into prayer.

One night, I was getting ready for bed when I felt this familiar tightness, this tingling in my heart, and I got up to pray. A couple of hours later, the daughter of a family friend called to say that she had been at a birthday party with her girlfriends. She told her friends that she felt like they should leave. When her friends would not consent, she went outside and called a cab to take her home. Soon after that, a fight broke out at the party. One of her girlfriends, who had refused to leave with her, was pushed, fell down a flight of stairs, and hurt her leg and ankle. She stated it was as if someone knew that she was in trouble and was praying for her. She said she remembered that she saw me in a quick glance like I was looking straight at her right before she felt the urge to leave the party. This was the hand of God moving to prevent her from getting hurt.

By the way, there is something that I would like for you to abide by. When faced with a storm, praying for others is a great and rewarding remedy. And here is some great news for you: there is such tremendous joy in helping others, despite our own situations, that we will cover this topic in another chapter of this book.

In the natural realm, before a storm comes, there are signs which make us want to prepare for the storm. We want to be under covering lest the storm finds us outside. We get candles and lamps in case the electricity goes out. We pile up extra blankets in case there is no heat. We want to make sure we are kept warm. We stock up on water because it is a necessary ingredient in our everyday life. We pick up medications, and in some US states, we board our windows and doors. Everything that we know to be necessary and lifesaving, we make sure that we possess them; they are in our home, close at hand, so that the storm does not find us unprepared. Moreover, we make sure that our family members are also covered and have the basic necessities for the storm.

I read an article online a while ago that gives step-by-step instructions on knowing if a storm is coming and what to do to prepare for the storm. I write it below.

1. Go outside.

2. Look at the sky (away from the sun).

3. If the sky is blue, and the clouds are white and moving fast, normal, then probably there won't be a storm.

4. If you see any of the following signs: a dark rolling cloud moving fast, hear thunder, spot lightning, hear a storm siren, catch a glimpse of a tornado, rain, hail, or steel, a storm is here, and you need to take precautionary actions to find shelter. It says to hurry inside somewhere and stay inside until the storm stops. Ensure that your family is also sheltered during the storm.

In the same manner, our Father in heaven knows when our storm is approaching and encourages us to take shelter in Him. At times, we receive warning signs. We failed sometimes to pay attention to a dream, a feeling, a word from God, a word from a trusted friend, a word from a prophet of God. In the same manner that you rush to take cover during a physical, natural storm, when you know that you are in a spiritual storm, take cover at our Father's house. He is your shelter. Psalm 91:1 (ESV) says, "He who dwells in the shelter of the most High will abide in the shadow of the Almighty." God prepared spiritual weapons available to us to fight in a storm. When the devil wants you to lose your sanity, when you feel like you are bordering on being irrational, God has ammunitions at your disposal to win the battle.

ARE YOU GOING THROUGH A STORM OF DESTRUCTION?

Sometimes, we wait too long before shifting into action when we are in a storm. We neglect to nip it in the bud at the onset. If only we had put our hands out and said, "Hey, don't even try that with me; don't come any closer; I am God's property." According to the Word of God, the stage that you are in as far as your storm will determine the weapons that you use. Mark 9:29 (ESV) says, "And he said to them, 'This kind cannot be driven out by anything but prayer.'" If your storm is making you feel totally overwhelmed, the devil has managed to downright bind you. You are in a pit so deep you don't know if you will find your way out. The steps up look steep to you. You are inclined to think that you are in a state of hopelessness; it will take some heavy-duty prayers to break you out of that situation. Do you follow me so far? If you go into the battle feeling defeated, then so you will be. I want you to know even if you failed to stop the attack when it first began, God is still able to get you out of the storm. It is never too late with God. He is a faithful God. That, you can count on.

SPIRITUAL WEAPONS

Here is some great news for you: we are blessed to serve a Mighty God who provides us with powerful weapons and tactics to fight our battles and carry us through the storms. "Blessed be the Lord, my rock, who trains my hands for war, and my fingers for battle" (Psalm 144:1, ESV).

1. *The Word of God* can never fail. The promises
   of God are true. I remember one man that I
   mentored; Freddie was his name. When he first
   came to know the Lord, Freddie thought that
   as soon as he walked to the altar and accepted
   Christ, all of his problems and addictions would
   immediately go away. He was very surprised
   when he went home that day to realize that his
   problems were still there waiting for him. As he
   shared with me his disbelief and even his failing
   faith, he expressed to me that his preconceived
   idea was that he should no longer be fighting
   his battles. I explained to him about the Word
   of God and His promises to us, His children.
   One of the CDs I gave him to listen to was a
   song called "Standing on the Promises of God."

Freddie and I had many other conversations during this trying time in his life. Years later, he called me, and as we were speaking, he told me that the important thing that really got him through those times was knowing the promises of God and the song "Standing on the Promises of God." He said that he would listen to the song repeatedly. He received the strength he wanted from understanding that he needed to stand, and he did. The song goes like this:

> Standing on the promises of Christ, my King,
> Through eternal ages, let his praises ring.
> Glory in the highest, I will shout and sing,
> Standing on the promises of God.
>
> (Refrain)
>
> Standing, standing,
> Standing on the promises of Christ, my Savior.
> Standing, standing,
> I'm standing on the promises of God.
>
> Standing on the promises that cannot fail,
> When the howling storms of doubt and fear assail,
> By the living Word of God, I shall prevail,
> Standing on the promises of God.
>
> (Refrain)
>
> Standing on the promises of Christ the Lord,
> Bound to him eternally by love's strong cord,
> Overcoming daily with the Spirit's sword,
> Standing on the promises of God.
>
> (Refrain)

Standing on the promises I cannot fall,
Listening every moment to the Spirit's call,
Resting in my Savior as my all in all,
Standing on the promises of God.

(Refrain)

Take the Bible, then go over the scriptures in the category of what you are dealing with. Then, pray through those verses. There are over 7,000 Bible promises that come directly from our Lord and Savior! See them as a credit card with no spending limit, and the best part is you do not need to pay back (no bill collectors will run up your cellular phone bill or call your home) except by your love, trust, and obedience. So, charge away at those verses; see His love is directing you. Take it as I say: as a gift card, all you need to do is redeem it, and God will always come true for you.

This is the right way to use God's building materials so that your home will become stormproof. Therefore, when the storms come, you will ride them out to be better, stronger, and more content; you will ride them to become the person Christ called you to be. You will develop the tenacity, the will, and the inner strength that our Father intended in His mercy for you to have to withstand the calamities, disasters, tests, and trials of life.

Whether you are new in the faith or an old timer, it is always good to know and/or to be reminded of the promises that God made to us and believe and rest on the promises of God. We need to pray according to the Word of God, according to the promises of God. First John 5:14 (ESV) says, "And this is the confidence that we have toward him, that if we ask anything according to his will he hears us." God is in the details. Have specific prayer points that you want to use when you pray. Set aside time to pray and spend time in the presence of the Lord. Fast and concentrate on hearing from your Father in heaven. If you are new to the faith or don't know how to pray, there are some specific prayers in the books of the Bible according to the storm you are facing. There are some scriptures that apply to each situation, for example, children, financial problems, relationships, marriage, trials, sickness, and so much more.

1. *Prayer Warriors*:

Have you heard of this term before, prayer warrior? Intercessors? For a couple of years, I led an intercessory prayer team at a church that I used to attend. They had two (2) services every Sunday morning. I would attend one of the services, and for the duration of the other service, I would lead a team of prayer warriors to intercede for the church and the entire church service. We would enter the prayer room and start praying for the church, go from one point to the other, and intercede for the leaders, the members, and all that would come and ask for prayer. We would go over the Sunday bulletin and notice the information for the day, the sick, the shut-in, and we would travail before the Throne of Grace until we saw the results. We would go before God and plead for every event and for everyone and everything in that church. Prayer warriors are trusted individuals who have a relationship with Jesus Christ that you can share your storm with. They would travail for you before the Throne of Grace, stay connected to you, and pray with you until victory is achieved. As prayer warriors, we could not share the information or prayer requests that were made to us. We only interceded for the needs of the church, the leaders, the people, and for God's will to be established in that church. Prayer warriors are compassionate people who want to see you come out on top and celebrate your victory. When I attended one of Benny Hinn's meetings in New Jersey, his man in charge asked whether anyone in the building would like to come and join the intercessory team and spend the time praying for a mighty move of God. That night, I left my seat and went to pray. What a rewarding experience!

When you are going through a storm, you need to surround yourself with prayer warriors. I have to tell you that the term "prayer warrior" is not found in scripture, but a prayer warrior is someone—a Christian—who prays effectively and continually for others according to the Word of God, in the power of the Holy Ghost and in the name of Jesus. To be a prayer warrior is to engage in someone's spiritual battle and fight the good fight of faith on their behalf. Prayer warriors usually have a heart for God, a heart for prayer, a heart for the people of God, and a heart to want to see them healed, delivered, transformed, and restored according to the Scriptures. More important than that, to be a prayer warrior, you have to have a relationship with Jesus Christ. Here is an exercise for you: after you read this, locate the prayer warriors in your environment, in your church, and in your life.

2. *Praise and Worship*:

The Bible says that the Lord inhabits the praises of the people. "But thou art holy, O thou that inhabits the praises of Israel" (Psalm 22:3, ASV).

There is something that praise does for one's soul. The dictionary defines praise as "the expression of approval or admiration for someone or something." It was A. B. Simpson who said, and I quote, "When you cannot rejoice in feelings, circumstances, or conditions, rejoice in the Lord. Praise God with all that you have." In the Old Testament, "The Lord said to him [Moses], 'What is that in your hand?' 'A staff,' he [Moses] replied'" (Exodus 4:2, NIV). Use the weapons that you have in your hands in a storm. Use your voice to sing praises to the Lord. Get some praise CDs and listen to them in your house. Nowadays, with the expansion of technology, you can buy songs online for as little as 99 cents and be able to download them immediately on your device. Let the praises of the Lord permeate your house, your entire being, and receive from the Lord. David danced before the Lord. Second Samuel 6:14 (CSB) states, "David was dancing with all his might before the LORD wearing a linen ephod." Praise is such an important weapon at your disposal that we will spend more time discussing it in another chapter.

3. *The Whole Armor of God*:

Ephesians 6:10–18 gives us a summary of what it takes to receive our victory and to remain triumphant. Do you want a victory? Do you want to come out on top? Do you want to have insights into the Word and the promises of God and be ready and equipped for every battle that would come your way? Then:

> Finally, be strong in the Lord and in his mighty power. Put on the full armor of God, so that you can take your stand against the devil's schemes. For our struggle is not against flesh and blood, but against the rulers, against the authorities, against the powers of this dark world and against the spiritual forces of evil in the heavenly realms. Therefore put on the full armor of God, so that when the day of evil comes, you may be able to stand your ground, and after you have done everything, to stand. Stand firm then, with the belt of truth buckled around your waist, with the breastplate of righteousness in place, and with your feet fitted with the readiness that comes from the gospel of peace. In addition to all this, take up the shield of faith, with which you can extinguish all the flaming arrows of the evil one. Take the helmet of salvation and the sword of the Spirit, which is the Word of God." And pray in the Spirit on all occasions with all kinds of prayers and requests. With this in mind, be alert and always keep on praying for all the Lord's people.

EPHESIANS 6:10–18 (NIV)

35

Let me tell you, we need every piece of the armor of God. The Bible makes us understand that there are six main pieces to this armor. Apostle Paul says that we are to have our "loins girt about with truth, we are to put on "the breastplate of righteousness" and our feet are to be shod with "the preparation of the gospel of peace." Then, we are to take up "the shield of faith," to put on "the helmet of salvation," and to use "the sword of the Spirit." Those are the six pieces of the armor mentioned. Apostle Paul does not mean this list to be exhaustive. There are evidently other aspects to spiritual warfare and to our resistance, as we have been discussing. What Apostle Paul did for us was to pick out some important pieces, which are absolutely essential as we look at battles, storms, and spiritual warfare in general. Many commentators of the Bible agree that these six pieces of armor can be classified into two (2) groups of three (3) each. The foundation of this division is roughly that the first three (3) are parts that are actually fixed on our body. The girdle about the loins, for instance, is actually fixed in position on the body. So is the breastplate. They do not hang loosely on our bodies. They must be tied or braced on. The sandals, likewise, have to be fixed firmly upon the feet. These three parts of the armor have that feature in common. But when you come to the shield, you are dealing with something that is not fastened securely on the body, as is the helmet. The helmet in the days of Apostle Paul was not fixed onto the head as it is done today.

The order in which the pieces are mentioned is also of importance and significance. Apostle Paul did not write down these items at random or as he looked at a soldier; he actually built a case for us, and it is important that we adopt his method and look at these parts of the armor separately. We need every piece of the armor of God in our everyday life. Apostle Paul would not have detailed this for us in the Word if he had not considered them to be important in our walk as Christians. Let's take a closer look at each piece.

If we look at history, in the ancient world, a soldier's belt not only kept his armor in place, but it would be wide enough, as a girdle, to protect his kidneys and other vital organs, just as the truth protects us. Practically applied to us today, you could say that the belt of truth holds us up spiritually so that we do not find ourselves exposed and susceptible to attacks or harm in virtually every area of our lives that matters.

Jesus said that Satan is the "father of lies," and

dishonesty is one of the enemy's oldest tactics, which he still uses today. We can discover Satan's lies by holding them against the truth of the Bible. Is it biblical? The truth of God's Word shines its light of integrity in our lives and holds together all our spiritual fortifications. Remember, Satan wants you to stay focused on your storm; God wants you to focus on your victory and the rewards of the storm. Anyone or anything that you are primarily completely focused on will become your master and control you. If you keep your focus on God, then you will be able to master your storms and your problems and be victorious.

Jesus said in the book of John 14:6 (ESV), "I am the way and the truth and the life. No one comes to the Father except through me."

A wound to the chest can be fatal; we all know that. That's why soldiers in ancient times used to wear a breastplate to cover their hearts and lungs. I am positive that you've seen them in movies. You have heard them discussed when people have received gunshots to the chest. Our heart is so susceptible to the wickedness of this world, but our protection is the breastplate of righteousness, and that uprightness comes only from our Savior Jesus Christ. We cannot become righteous through our own virtuous works. When Jesus died on the cross for us, His righteousness was credited to all who believed in Him through justification. God sees us as sinless because of what His only begotten Son did for us. You need to accept your Christ-given righteousness. Let Christ's righteousness shelter and guard you. Remember to keep your heart pure and strong for God. I heard a sermon one time from a pastor who titled it "Our Heart, The Black Box" and talked about how important it is to keep our hearts pure, clean, and free of bitterness and resentment. Romans 4:3 (NIV) says, "What does Scripture say?" Abraham believed God, and it was credited to him as righteousness." Abraham was found to be a righteous man because of God. In the same manner, when God looks at us, what He sees is the blood of Jesus covering us, not our worthlessness. The blood of Jesus is, therefore, our covering and permits God to be able to look at us.

Ephesians 6:15 talks about fitting our feet with the readiness that comes from the gospel of peace. Satan propagates traps for us as we are trying to spread the gospel. The gospel of peace is our fortification, reminding us that it is by grace that souls are saved. The will of God will never take you where the grace of God will not protect you. We can avoid Satan's interferences when we remember that "For God so loved the world that he gave his one and only Son, that whoever believes in him shall not perish but have eternal life" (John 3:16, ESV). The gospel that we have is the good news that God purchased peace by the death of His Son, Jesus Christ, and offers it to all sinners who believe in Him.

We have the good news that God's inevitable wrath against sinners has been done away with through the death of Jesus Christ, His Son, who died for our sins. Everyone who believes is reconciled to Him freely by grace, not by works. Hence, in the place of enmity comes divine peace. There is nothing more wonderful in the entire world than to be at peace with God. Are you at peace with God? With all men?

Fitting our feet with the readiness of the gospel of peace is described in 1 Peter 3:15 (NKJV) like this: "Always be ready to give a defense to everyone who asks you a reason for the hope that is in you, with meekness and fear." As we share the gospel of salvation, we ultimately bring about peace between God and men. Are you at peace? With God? With men?

A shield is an important defensive armor. The shield was responsible for fending off arrows, spears, and swords. Our shield of faith guards us against one of

Satan's deadliest weapons: doubt. Satan throws doubt at us when God does not act immediately or in the way we expect. But our faith in God's trustworthiness and willingness to hear from His children comes from the unquestionable truth of the Bible. We know our Father can be counted on. The Bible says He is not a man that He shall lie. "God is not a man, so he does not lie. He is not human, so he does not change his mind. Has he ever spoken and failed to act? Has he ever promised and not carried it through?" (Numbers 23:19, NLT). Our shield of faith sends Satan's fiery arrows of doubt, glancing meaninglessly to the side. We keep our shield held high, self-assured in the awareness and protection that God provides. God protects, and God is faithful to His children. Our shield holds because of the One our faith is in, who is Jesus Christ, the Son of the Living God.

The **helmet of salvation** protects the head, where all thought and knowledge reside. Jesus Christ said, "If you hold to my teaching, you are really my disciples. Then you will know the truth, and the truth will set you free" (John 8:31–32, NIV). The truth of salvation through Christ does indeed set us free. Those who reject God's plan of salvation fight Satan unprotected and suffer the deadly blow of hell.

You cannot succeed without Christ. He is the Vine.

First Corinthians 2:16 tells us that believers "have the mind of Christ" (1 Corinthians 2:16, ESV). Even more interesting, 2 Corinthians 10:5 (NIV) explains that those who are in Christ have the divine power to "demolish arguments and every pretension that sets itself up against the knowledge of God, and we take captive every thought to make it obedient to Christ." The helmet of salvation protecting our thoughts and minds is such an essential piece of our armor. We will not be able to survive without it.

The **sword of the Spirit** is the only offensive weapon in the full armor of God with which we can strike against Satan. This weapon represents the Word of God, the Bible. "For the word of God is alive and active. Sharper than any double-edged sword, it penetrates even to dividing soul and spirit, joints and marrow; it judges the thoughts and attitudes of the heart" (Hebrews 4:12, NIV).

When Jesus was tempted in the desert by Satan, He refuted with the truth of Scripture, the Word of God, setting an example for us. Satan's strategies have not changed, so the sword of the Spirit, the Bible, is still our best defense. Commit the Word to your memory and to your heart. David said in Psalm

119:111 (ESV), "I have hidden your word in my heart that I might not sin against you."

Finally, Paul adds **the power of prayer** to the full armor of God: "And pray in the Spirit on all occasions with all kinds of prayers and requests. With this in mind, be alert and always keep on praying for the entire Lord's people" (Ephesians 6:18, NIV).

Every smart soldier knows they must keep the line of communication open with their commander. God has instructions for us through His Word and the promptings of the Holy Spirit. Satan hates it when we pray. He knows prayer strengthens us and keeps us alert to his deception, distraction, and confusion. Apostle Paul cautions us to pray for others as well. With the full armor of God and the ability to pray, we can be ready for whatever the enemy throws at us; we can be ready and prepare for any storm that comes our way.

PRAYER

Listening to the Word of God is the key to power in prayer.

Be careful what you do when you enter the house of God. Some fools go there to offer sacrifices, even though they haven't sinned. But it's best just to listen when you go to worship. Don't talk before you think or make promises to God without thinking them through. God is in heaven, and you are on earth, so don't talk too much.

ECCLESIASTES 5:1–2 (CEV)

Real prayer is not filled with pointless phrases but is the overspill of a heart filled with God's presence and abundance. You will know that your Father is present when your heart begins to melt. Tears begin to flow down your cheeks. Suddenly, every plain word begins to be filled with life. The Holy Spirit enters the room and is now directing and leading your prayers, aiming them at specific targets and leading you on the prayers and intercessions needed. Glory! It is like a commander who is gently stirring a boat, not to hurt it but firmly and lovingly bringing it to port and anchoring it. You feel yourself depending on the Holy Spirit to take you deeper into the presence of God as tears continue to flow down your face.

You experience this sweet presence just letting you know that your Father loves you and you are surrounded by His love, and you say, "What a joy I am in with my Father." You have entered the Holy of Holies, the third realm of prayer. You no longer need to struggle with your prayers; everything that you want to say just emanates from your lips. You cry out to your Father to help you, to keep you, to cover you. You are uttering specific requests to your Father, and you know that He is listening and paying attention to you. You leave your place of prayer feeling strengthened, feeling like your relationship with your Heavenly Father has become deeper and that you have experienced and met God. This is the prayer that touches our Father. You sense that you no longer need to fear or be troubled. Your Father in heaven has you in the palm of His hands, and you are safe. He is such a place of safety and security. The Bible says that He is our refuge, an ever-present help in times of danger, our strong tower. Cry unto Him in the days of troubles, and He will deliver you (Psalm 50:15). You will give Him thanks. You begin to thank God for this time of fellowship with Him. You do not want to let this moment go. You want to hold on to it, this cherished and intimate moment with your Father. You understand that your Father knows where you are, and He knows that you will overcome this storm, and now you know it also. Andrew Murray, a great man of God, said that before he adorned himself to prayer, he would always ask God to melt his heart and break him. Brokenness before God touches the heart of our Father. It is a prerequisite to our answers to prayer. Are you broken? Broken before your Father in heaven and not before men? Then, you are a candidate to be used by God. God bless you.

THE MINDSET IN THE FIGHT

You must prepare yourself mentally, emotionally, and spiritually. When the devil throws the first punch, if you drop yourself on the floor, you are defeated. You have allowed him to win the first round and made the remaining of the fight more difficult. Don't get me wrong, I know it is not easy to feel spiritually under attack. I have dealt with so many tests and trials in my life. What I am trying to do is to help you gain a better understanding of the storms and give you spiritual tactics to alleviate your battles. Use specific prayer points; aim your prayer at your target.

If you are telling yourself that you don't see how you will get out of that situation, if you are now telling God that you will never make it, stop it right now. If you are dealing with the loss of a job and convincing yourself that you will not be able to find a job, you might find yourself all alone, having a pity party. No, stand up, bring your best out, do not give up, stand. Ephesians 6:14 (RSV) says, "Therefore take the whole armor of God, that you may be able to withstand in the evil day, and having done all, to stand." *Stand*.

SPEAK WITH CONFIDENCE!

There is a scripture in the book of Job that really speaks to my heart. It states, "You will also decree a thing, and it will be established for you" (Job 22:28, NKJV). Someone has said it is not everybody whom the devil attacks—some people, he would not dare to attack because he knows their spiritual strength. Some people have worked on strengthening their inner man to make themselves less susceptible to devilish attacks and manipulations. The devil likes to take advantage of weak people; he likes to attack the complainers, the wimps. Have confidence in the God that you serve. He is everything you need. He is a doctor in the emergency room. He is a physician in the sick room. He is a teacher in the classroom. He is a banker in the finance room. And He is a defender in the courtroom. He is everything to us. Keep your mind focused on Jesus. He is the "Author and Finisher of all things." If you keep your mind and your eyes focused on the storm, you lose the battle. I am sure that you heard the saying, "Don't overwhelm God with your problems; overwhelm your problems with God." Don't keep telling God how big your problems are; instead, tell your problems how big your God is. He can sustain you. He has declared in His Word that you are "more than conquerors" (Romans 8:37, CEV), the "head, not the tail." Your joy originates from a life consumed with purpose and focused on Jesus.

Remember that God also uses problems to lead you in the right direction. You will be tested. You will go to trials, and if your faith is found to be unwavering, then nothing can stand in your way.

Sometimes, God needs to smack us in the face to wake us up. Without such wake-up calls, we will blindly fall onto the wrong path, which would lead to greater disappointment and ruin. We will not see it coming because our will is hindering His. But know this: God is there governing and protecting us, even when we do not see Him. And be warned, if your will is obstructing His will, He will light a fire under you to get you moving. If He did not, you would be left to your own destruction, and it would demonstrate a lack of love. In the book of Exodus, we see that, at one point, God wanted to exterminate the children of Israel and see Moses's response to God. We read,

> "I have seen these people," the Lord said to Moses, "and they are a stiff-necked people. Now leave me alone so that my anger may burn against them and that I may destroy them. Then I will make you into a great nation." But Moses sought the favor of the Lord his God. "Lord," he said, "why should your anger burn against your people, whom you brought out of Egypt with great power and a mighty hand? Why should the Egyptians say, 'It was with evil intent that he brought them out, to kill them in the mountains and to wipe them off the face of the earth'? Turn from your fierce anger; relent and do not bring disaster on your people. Remember your servants Abraham, Isaac and Israel, to whom you swore by your own self: 'I will make your descendants as numerous as the stars in the sky and I will give your descendants all this land I promised them, and it will be their inheritance forever.'" Then the Lord relented and did not bring on his people the disaster he had threatened.
>
> **EXODUS 32:9–14 (NIV)**

Just as a parent will discipline their child out of love, God disciplines His children whom He loves. Problems will point us in the right direction if we surrender our will to His. His love is there to motivate and change us into the best path and plan, much better than we could ever imagine. Is God trying to get your attention?

Sometimes, it takes a painful situation to make us change our ways. "Blows and wounds scrub away evil, and beatings purge the inmost being" (Proverbs 20:30, NIV).

TELL IT TO THE MOUNTAIN!

When Jesus was going to pray for Jairus's daughter, a twelve-year-old girl, the crowd was pressing Him. People were all around Him as He walked to Jairus's house. When He arrived there, He would not let anybody go in with Him except three of His disciples, Peter, John, and James, and the mother and father of the girl. You might wonder why. When you are going through a storm, who do you trust to share your problems with? Do you know who your real friends are? Can you make the difference between friends and acquaintances? Do you know the real men and women of God who are able to hear your problems without spreading rumors? Some people want to divulge their problems so much that they make it a prayer point in a church service or in a prayer meeting. For instance, "Let us pray for sister so-and-so whom the husband beat up so badly that she had to spend two nights in the hospital and now is in a shelter for battered women, and her children are with her mother." Do you know anybody like that? You might share your storm with someone who would go and broadcast it all over town, making it worse for you.

Growing up, we knew a little lady, our neighbor, whom we all called Channel 5 because she would broadcast to the whole neighborhood any confidential information that she gathered. And if someone confronted her, her excuse would be, "Why did you tell me your problems? You know that I would share it." Some of your friends are unfriendly friends. They are the ones who are helping you pray but wishing you would fail; secretly, they wish you would not make it. Negative-minded people in your environment will push you to also be thinking negatively. Some people have nothing to give except to share their pessimistic views of your problems. The Bible is filled with examples. First Corinthians 15:33 (ESV) states, "Do not be deceived: 'Bad Company corrupts good morals.'" Do you recall Job's friends in the book of Job when Job was going through the storm of his life? Were they encouraging? Let's look. Eliphaz states in Job 4:7–8 (NIV), "Remember: who that was innocent ever perished? Or where were the upright cut off? As I have seen, those who plow iniquity and sow trouble reap the same." What does he mean by that?

He is saying that Job's suffering must be because of some iniquity or sin in his life. In this case, we know that Job was not being judged or punished for any type of sin; in fact, it was quite the contrary. Eliphaz's opinion of Job's problems was not accurate. Some church folks will pass judgment on you as easily as putting their clothes on after a shower; others are immature in the faith and will not understand the work of God in your life. Above all things, my advice to you is to "stand."

The second friend, Bildad, gets straight to the point when he begins his speech. The Bible says:

> How long will you say these things, and the words of your mouth be a great wind? Does God pervert justice? Or does the Almighty pervert the right? If your children have sinned against him, he has delivered them into the hand of their transgression. If you will seek God and plead with the Almighty for mercy, if you are pure and upright, surely then he will rouse himself for you and restore your rightful habitation.

> JOB 8:2–6 (ESV)

Bildad lays it out, saying that Job's kids were killed

because of their sin against God. He then tells Job what he thinks Job should do, which is to get on his face and plead for mercy! Bildad hears Job stating that he is blameless in all his suffering, and Bildad thinks his words are like a blustering wind! He does not believe it. Have you ever met some self-righteous Christian who felt like they knew everything and would not listen to reason or see the obvious?

Finally, his third friend, Zophar, expressed an opinion.

Are all these words to go unanswered? Is this talker to be vindicated? Will your idle talk reduce others to silence? Will no one rebuke you when you mock? You say to God, "My beliefs are flawless, and I am pure in your sight." Oh, how I wish that God would speak, that he would open his lips against you and disclose to you the secrets of wisdom, for true wisdom has two sides. Know this: God has even forgotten some of your sin. Can you fathom the mysteries of God? Can you probe the limits of the Almighty? They are higher than the heavens above— what can you do? They are deeper than the depths below—what can you know? Their measure is longer than the earth and wider than the sea. If he comes along and confines you in prison and convenes a court, who can oppose him? Surely, he recognizes deceivers; and when he sees evil, does he not take note? But the witless can no more become wise than a wild donkey's colt can be born a human being.

JOB 11:2–12 (NIV)

53

Zophar's speech really baffled me. He basically tells him that he must have sin in his life, and he wishes that God would come down and tell it to him as it is. Really, Zophar calls him unwise and, at that point, tells him how good it is to get right with God. So, these three (3) friends of Job were quick to make assumptions about why Job was having trouble, and none of them were right. If they were praying for him, I have to say that their prayer points would not have been to the point. Now remember that these three (3) men are Job's friends who know about what he is going through, but they are hasty to make suppositions about his trials. They are looking at him sitting on the ashes because of his pain as they are expressing their opinions of his difficulties. There is a saying that goes, "With friends like these, who needs enemies?" Have you heard of it before?

Some people in your environment right now are not your real friends. You need to pray and ask God for discernment in choosing your friend, your prayer partners, and the people that you would share your problems with. A while back, when I first came to the United States, I went to visit some of my family members in Florida. They were so excited to see me; in fact, they wanted me to move to Florida to be with them. They started introducing me to many of the people that they knew. They finally introduced me to a group of friends whom they told me owned the town. By that, I mean those were the people to know; they were involved in businesses, the who's who at the time. They asked this group of people to break me in and show me around while I was there. They trusted these people completely and were hoping that I would also make them my friends. As I came to know the people in question, I realized that this group of people was very deceitful, even within themselves. Although they seemed to be very friendly with each other, they were at each other's throats. Competition and jealousy were the name of the game. They would criticize and gossip about each other every chance they got. No one was exempt. They would try to encroach on each other. Soon, they would each try to speak to me separately, and every time, they would speak badly about one another.

They thrived on gossip, on competition, and on wicked assumptions and evil schemes. They were all making the same ignorant statements about each other, how no one should trust the other. I realized that on the outside, this circle of friends looked respectful, friendly, engaging, and prominent, ready to help, but what was going on inside was nothing less than a ring of devils. So many people swear by this circle, this clique. If you did not know them or were not included in the circle, you felt left out. Fans were fighting just to be added to their list of acquaintances. When I noticed so many inconsistencies between who these people portrayed themselves to be and who they really were, I started praying, asking God to reveal more to me.

Wait! There is more. One day, I was speaking to one of them when he told me not to accept or consume any food from another one because he was a voodoo priest. Now, I don't know for you, but I always thought that if I ever met a voodoo priest, I would identify him as such because he would dress dirty, his language would be particular, and there would be outward signs to me that this person is involved in witchcraft. This person did not fit my description of a voodoo priest. You can imagine my disbelief and my shock upon receiving this piece of information. My mind was racing. Keeping my emotions under control and doing my best not to show that I was stunned, I started asking questions about the other ones and finally asked him about himself. He told me that he himself was a voodoo priest and a Freemason but that he only practiced it for himself, his family, and his close friends. I found out that day that this circle of friends that a whole community was admiring, putting on a pedestal, imitating, and submitting to was a ring of adulterers, Freemasons, voodoo priests, drinkers, gossipers, manipulators, and unreliable people. They were also sons of witches and wizards, and some of them had been dedicated to the devil by their Satan-worshiper parents. Getting myself out was not easy; it took God's intervention to separate me from that circle of unfriendly friends, that ring of devils, but we serve an Almighty God. Are you with me?

If you are reading this book, chances are you are going through a storm or someone you know is in a battle, and you want to get information on how to help them. I encourage you to take a good look at the people around you, examine and pray to God to know if you are in a circle with friends or in a ring of devils. Knowing the difference can save your life. I hate to say this, but in my life, I have also encountered, because of my unquestioning and, at that time, naïve character, many men and women of God who were involved in demonic manipulations. When they were ministering, they looked as if the anointing flowing was from heaven, but upon closer investigation and revelation, I had to come to the realization that these pastors, apostles, and bishops were deeply involved with the kingdom of darkness and pulling their powers from that source instead of God. Again, God, in His mercy, had to take me out from under their satanic manipulations. It is my prayer that God will touch their hearts and that they will change their ways. I am sharing these experiences with you to remind you that the Bible asks us to be vigilant. Pray for the people in your environment. Ask God for mercy and revelation knowledge of the people who should be praying with you and for you and the people whom you share your trials with. When in a storm, we tend to be vulnerable and, therefore, susceptible to the manipulations and crafty devices of the enemy. I will talk more about this subject matter in my book *My Life, My Love, My Prayer.*

CHAPTER 2:

YOUR FAITH IS ALL GOD NEEDS

I want to let you in on a little secret: God does not need your help. He is God all by Himself. He is the Creator of everything that exists and existed before the creation of time. He is creation's Creator. He is the Alpha and the Omega. The Bible says, "He knows the end from the beginning." Isaiah 46:10 (NLT) states, "Only I can tell you the future before it even happens. Everything I plan will come to pass, for I do whatever I wish." He is able to get you out of any storms ravaging your life right now. What He needs from you is your faith to accomplish it. Faith is such an important factor in the life of a Christian. Hebrews 11:1 (ESV) states, "Now faith is the assurance of things hoped for, the conviction of things not seen." The most popular version of this verse is King James, which I am positive that you have heard before: "Now faith is the substance of things hoped for, the evidence of things not seen" (Hebrews 11:1, KJV). Faith is the foundation of our hope. What the writer of the book of Hebrews is trying to relate to us is that faith is the groundwork of confidence for everything that we are hoping for. Faith is the road on which your hope travels to reach your goal. Let's expound on the meaning of the word "faith." Thayer's Greek Lexicon defines "faith" as "the conviction of the truth of anything, belief." When it relates to God, faith is the conviction that God exists and is the Creator and ruler of all things, the provider and bestower of eternal salvation through Christ.

Adam Clarke's Commentary defines the word "substance" as what a foundation becomes for another thing to stand on. I pray that these explanations give you a better understanding of the word "faith" and how you can allow your life to be transformed on a daily basis if you are willing to take on the challenge of this perpetual journey of faith and hope in the one true God. Habakkuk 2:4 and Romans 1:17 (KJV) say, "But the just shall live by faith." And you ask, "Why should it be so important for the just to live by faith?" The answer lies in the Bible in the book of Hebrews Chapter 11, verse 6 (NLT): "And it is impossible to please God without faith. Anyone who wants to come to him must believe that God exists and that He rewards those who sincerely seek him." When we do not believe or when we stop believing in God to help us out of any storm, trial, or test, it is like we are saying to Him, "You are not big enough. You are not powerful enough." Remember I told you in the previous chapter to stop telling God how big your problem is but instead speak to your storm and let it know how big your God is. God says in the book of Jeremiah 33:3 (NIV), "Call to me and I will answer you and tell you great and unsearchable things you do not know."

For all these reasons, if we are going to go anywhere in God and walk victoriously, it will be by our faith in the Son of God. Faith is the expectation of what God has promised the believer in Christ, and hope accepts it. The Bible says that "Faith comes by hearing and hearing the Word of God" (Romans 10:17, KJV). The Amplified Version states, "So faith comes by hearing [what is told], and what is heard comes by the preaching [of the message that came from the lips] of Christ (the Messiah Himself)" (Romans

10:17, AMP). But that is not all; our original faith, which is our saving faith, came from Jesus Christ and was imparted into us to bring us to the Lord. We know that Jesus Christ is the Author and Finisher of our faith according to Hebrews 12:2. An author is an originator or a creator. The Greek word "author" in Hebrews 12:2 can also be translated as "captain" or "chief leader." From that, we can arrive at the deduction that Jesus Christ is the originator of our faith in that He started it as well as is the captain of our faith. It all comes down to this: Jesus Christ is also the one who maintains our faith. He controls it and keeps it safe as a captain watches over and steers his boat.

Moreover, Romans 12:3 (NKJV) states, "For through the grace given to me I say to everyone among you not to think more highly of himself than he ought to think; but to think so as to have sound judgment, as God has allotted to each a measure of faith." Can you see how great that is? The Greek word for "perfecter" can literally be translated as "finisher," "completer." It appears only once in the Bible in Hebrews 12:2 and speaks about bringing something to its conclusion. This is something to keep in mind. In other words, Jesus both creates and withstands our faith. I told you earlier about receiving the saving faith. Jesus, consequently, is the Sustainer of our faith. In reality, this is the basis of great security to us in times of struggle, in times of spiritual warfare, and when we are going through life storms.

FAITH IS ACTION

"But someone may well say, 'You have faith and I have works.' Show me your faith without the works, and I will show you my faith by my works" (James 2:18, ESV). Faith is action. Faith is perfected by works. "Was Abraham our father not justified by works when he offered Isaac his son on the altar? Do you see that faith was working together with his works, and by works faith was made perfect?" (James 2:21–22, ESV). Faith cannot exist without being active in works of righteousness. His faith in God would have been of no benefit to him if it had not manifested through works. Adam Clarke's Commentary states that even true faith will soon die if the possessor does not live in the spirit of obedience.

When we read the book of Hebrews, we are presented with many figures of faith; many personalities of the Bible are mentioned relating to their faith. The other thing that we noticed is that each one of them mentioned is described in terms of an action. An amazing story is the story of Noah; he built an ark. Abraham left his home, Jacob blessed his grandsons, Joseph instructed about his bones, Moses chose to be mistreated, and Joshua fought. Faith is synonymous with action. Apart from action, there is no faith. In fact, I can tell you that faith does not exist in a noun form in Hebrew. It is only expressed as a verb because it indicates action. Faith is a conviction expressed in a choice. It starts with belief, but if this belief does not take sustenance in obedience, it is not yet faith. Faith is belief in action; can I say that? Have you ever started something that you believed you wanted to do, but when it came down to it, you changed your mind? This looks like the approach that a lot of people take on faith. They believed, but they failed to act on that belief. If you believe, act upon it. That is faith.

Faith is not believing that God will sustain you, but it is, as they say, to let go and let God. It is leaning on Him, expecting Him to hold on to you. I report this poem that many of us grew up with, the painting of it on the walls of our homes.

"FOOTPRINTS IN THE SAND"
by Carolyn Carty (1963)

One night, a man had a dream.
He dreamed He was walking along the beach with the LORD.
Across the sky flashed scenes from His life.
For each scene, he noticed two sets of footprints in the sand.
One belonging to him and the other to the LORD.

When the last scene of His life flashed before Him,
He looked back at the footprints in the sand.
He noticed that many times along the path of His life,
There was only one set of footprints.
He also noticed that it happened at the very lowest and
saddest times of his life.

This really bothered him, and he questioned the LORD
about it.
"LORD, You said that once I decided to follow You,
You'd walk with me all the way.
But I have noticed that during the most troublesome times in
my life,
There is only one set of footprints.
I don't understand why, when I needed You most, You would
leave me."

The LORD replied, "My precious, precious child, I love you,
and I would never leave you!
During your times of trial and suffering,
When you see only one set of footprints, it was then that I
carried you."

Many people seem to think that faith is merely
a mental conviction, but for faith to be valid, it

requires action. It was by faith that Abel brought a more acceptable offering to God than Cain did. Abel's offering gave evidence that he was a righteous man, and God showed His approval of his gifts. Although Abel is long dead, he still speaks to us by his example of faith. Hebrews 11:4 tells us to please pay attention; Jesus Christ is not only the Instigator and Sustainer of our redeemable faith. He is also the Sustainer of our daily walk with God and the finisher of our divine journey. There is one thing I am sure of, "For I am confident of this very thing, that He who began a good work in you will perfect it until the day of Christ Jesus" (Philippians 1:6, NASB).

BE WILLING TO RECEIVE HELP FROM OTHERS

Don't isolate yourself. Christianity is not a solo sport; it is a team effort filled with relationships and opportunities. Find your support in a good and solid church family. If you are in a big church, get in a small group, do not be alone, and do not stay anonymous. Galatians 6:2 (KJV) says, "Bear ye one another's burdens, and so fulfil the law of Christ." Many Christians would be surprised to know that this verse is in the Bible. I state this as a matter of fact, but we live in a generation where even Christians no longer want to spend time in prayer for themselves, for their family, or for their pastors and friends. As Christians, we must be able to humble ourselves and ask for help when needed. Lean on your church family, for no man is an island.

DON'T TELL GOD... TELL THE DEVIL

Never tell God how big your storm is. He already knows. Tell your storm how big your God is. The Bible says in the book of Ephesians, "Together, we are his house, built on the foundation of the apostles and the prophets. And the cornerstone is Christ Jesus himself" (Ephesians 2:20, NLT). I can assure you that to get something you never had, you have to do something you never did. When God takes something from your grasp, He's not punishing you but merely opening your hands to receive something better. The will of God will never take you where the grace of God will not protect you. He wants you to stand strong, stand firm, and rely on His Word. The truth lies in His Word, and the truth that you know will set you free. That means what has taken root in your spirit, in your life, and manifested will set you free through Jesus Christ. Don't get me wrong, it might be hard for you to stand and tell the devil about your God, but as you continue to worship God and stand upon His Word, confidence will invade you, your inner man will be strengthened, and you will start to experience changes in your attitude. In the book of Luke 8:22–25, the disciples found themselves in a storm. But Jesus showed Himself to be the God who is bigger than our storms. How we see God is very important because our view of God determines how we view ourselves. As it turns out, the storm was not as big to Jesus as it was to the disciples, and even though the storm was above their heads, it was still under Jesus's feet.

> One day Jesus said to his disciples, "Let us go over to the other side of the lake." So, they got into a boat and set out. As they sailed, he fell asleep. A squall came down on the lake so that the boat was being swamped, and they were in great danger. The disciples went and woke him, saying, "Master, Master, we're going to drown!" He got up and rebuked the wind and the raging waters; the storm subsided, and all was calm. "Where is your faith?" he asked his disciples. In fear and amazement, they asked one another, "Who is this? He commands even the winds and the water, and they obey him."

LUKE 8:22–25 (NIV)

I told you before about the fear of snakes that paralyzed my life for a long time. In the early days when I first came to Christ, I had a dream. I saw that I had come out of my body, and I was going to heaven. I started on my way up through the high-rise buildings and through the clouds. I was going up, and I kept traveling up. At some point, I told myself that what I was seeing was so vast that I would not know which direction was heaven. I suddenly heard these angelic voices singing a song like I had never heard anybody sing before. The voices were angelic, and that beautiful melody was reaching up. I looked, and I saw what seemed to be a raft filled with beings dressed in white robes with a gold sash around their waists. They were beautiful, and the raft was traveling in the air. There was something like a rope around the raft, and the singers were all inside. It was going really fast. It went past me, and I understood that they were going to heaven, so I started following the beautiful sound of the music. They were singing, "Hallelujah, for the Lord God Almighty reigns." I have to tell you that, at times, I felt like I was getting lost. It was so vast. Then, I would listen attentively to the singing voices, and the angelic sound would direct me to the way they were going, and I would follow. I think that every time I seemed to be losing my way, I would see the raft just floating and going up. It was breathtaking. At some point, I traveled past certain tall buildings that looked to be incredibly high, and some people started throwing rocks at me. I then again listened to where the sound was coming from, and I followed. It was beautiful. Words cannot describe it. As I reached closer to heaven, a giant snake wrapped a part of his body around one of my legs and pulled me down. So I looked at the snake, and I said, "You are the snake that has been oppressing my life. I am going to heaven, and I am taking you up with me to be judged." I was struggling to go up because the snake at that point was pulling me down.

I managed to reach a place made of glass with glass doors. As I reached for the doors, I looked at my leg, and the snake had disappeared. I continued through the glass doors into heaven, and I met a woman. I told her that I was there because I wanted to see Jesus. She gestured to me to follow her. I followed her, and I reached a place where many men were sitting around a basin with their feet in what appeared to me to be water, like a sauna with steam. For you to go in, you had to go through what I could describe as a detector. You could not go into the basin without going under a portal. I found myself inside, and I thought that my feet would be wet, but they were not.

One of them stood up and bid me to follow him, and I did. He took me to a back room. I looked, and I saw a pile of what looked like millions of small snakes, very tiny creatures, and they were stuffed. The sweetest voice I could ever hear spoke to me and said, "This is the snake that you are so afraid of." From that day, I realized that the snake, although it looked enormous to me and petrifying, was but a tiny stuffed animal in the hands of our Lord. My own perception of that snake was making it look bigger than it really was, but God was much greater than that. What am I saying to you? Our trials, our tests, our storms, and our fears may appear intimidating to us, but in the eyes of the Lord, they are just mere inconveniences. If only you would allow yourself to see them the way that God sees them, it would make such a big difference in your life. The disciples thought the storm would kill them all, but Jesus was sleeping. He had no fear because He knew. It is my prayer for you the God Almighty will open your spiritual eyes to be able to see that "Greater is He that is in you."

We may never go through a storm on the Sea of

Galilee like the disciples, but we go through various storms of life. Your storm may be that someone you love has died unexpectedly, and you don't understand it. It may be your job that is not going the way it should. It could be betrayal from those you love. It could be those times when life has you so confused that you don't know where to turn or what to do. It could be those times when Satan is busy whispering in your ears, "It is of no use, it will not work, no matter what, well, give up now." It could be that moment that you find yourself attracted to a married man or a married woman, and although you know that it is impossible, your heart is refusing to let go, and you are in pain.

God has a plan. That is in His nature. He planned it from the beginning of time. What do you do when heartaches come knocking at your door, and you are overcome by despair and feelings of hopelessness? Remember that God has a plan, and His plan is bigger than any storm that you may be going through. God has never failed in His intentions. Take courage in this verse, Philippians 1:6 (NIV), "And I am certain that God, who began the good work within you, will continue his work until it is finally finished on the day when Christ Jesus returns."

The Bible says that Jesus was sleeping throughout the storm. The disciples assumed they were at the end, that the tempest was dreadful. Jesus was sleeping. Clearly, He was not troubled by the storm. The disciples could not change their situations, and it is the same for us. Have you ever wished that you could change your circumstances, but you could not? Our analysis of our storm is different than that of God. His interpretation is the best because the Bible says in the book of Isaiah 55:8 (NLT), "'My thoughts are nothing like your thoughts,' says the Lord. 'And my ways are far beyond anything you could imagine.'" When you are going through a storm, do you want to adopt God's interpretation of the storm or your own? God uses our storms to get us closer to Him. Wherever the storm has originated from, whatever the cause of our plights, the Word of God says, "You intended to harm me, but God intended it for good to accomplish what is now being done" (Genesis 50:19, NIV). God sees your storm as a means to strengthen and promote you. God wants you to use your storm to come to be closer to Him.

The Bible says the ship was filled with water. The storm had taken control of the ship. Sometimes, when you are going through a storm, it feels like this problem is absolutely overriding your life. You are no longer in control. The disciples feared the worst. What did they do? The right thing. They went to Jesus. They woke Him up. And Jesus arose from His sleep. God is never too asleep not to hear His children's cries. Psalm 121 says that He who watches over us will not slumber. Psalm 121:1–3 (KJV) says, "I will lift up my eyes unto the hills, from whence cometh my help. My help cometh from the LORD, which made heaven and earth... He will not suffer your foot to be moved: he that keep you will not slumber."

God hears us when we cry out to Him. "Call to me and I will answer you and tell you great and unsearchable things you do not know" (Jeremiah 33:3, NIV). I want you to know that Jesus's sleep is not like our own. He rebuked the wind and the storm, and immediately calm occurred. Before we go any further, let me set something straight: if God can command the wind and the storms, don't you think that He can control your storm? If God can have control over nature, I am certain that He can take care of your storm. There is no storm too big for God. Psalm 34:17 (NLT) states, "The Lord hears his people when they call to him for help. He rescues them from all their troubles." I can't say that I understand how God does it, but what I know is that He uses the mess in our lives and turns it into a message. He takes our tests and turns them into a testimony. Jesus asked, "Where is your faith?" (Luke 8:25, NLT). As I am asking you today, "Where is your faith?" is your faith in your own ability to withstand? Is your faith in your circumstances being right? Is your faith in the ability of other people to help you? Or is your faith in the desires of this life? Is your faith in your assets? I must tell you that your faith needs to be in Jesus Christ. There is life beyond any storms that you are going through right now, and if your faith is in Jesus Christ, you have already conquered. Romans 8:28 (NLT) states, "And we know that God causes everything to work together for the good of those who love God and are called according to his purpose for them." The pleasures of this life are short-lived. The stuff that money can buy does not fulfill. Make no blunder; only God will never leave you nor forsake you. In 1932, A. M. Overton wrote this poem that is still so relevant today:

> My Father's way may twist and turn,
> My heart may throb and ache,
> But in my soul I'm glad to know,
> He makes no mistakes,

My cherished plans may go astray,
My hopes may fade away,
But still I'll trust my Lord to lead,
For He doth know the way,

Though the night be dark and it may seem,
That day will never break,
I'll pin my faith, my all in Him,
He makes no mistake,

There's so much now I cannot see,
My eyesight's far too dim,
But come what may, I'll simply trust,
And leave it all to Him,

For by and by the mist will lift,
And plain it all He'll make,
Through all the way, though dark to me,
He made not one mistake.

Don't tell God that your storm is taking over; tell your storm that your Father in heaven is in control of your life and believe it to be true.

KEEP YOUR EYES FIXED ON HIM!

We do this by keeping our eyes on Jesus, the champion who initiates and perfects our faith. Because of the joy awaiting Him, He endured the cross, disregarding its shame. Now He is seated in the place of honor beside God's throne (Hebrews

12:2). Where do we find the strength to go through the storms of life? We look unto Jesus Christ in us. I believe that this statement should make you so content and confident that you need to just set the book on the table for a minute and give God the praise and thank Him. When Apostle Paul wrote the books of Ephesians, Philemon, Colossians, and Philippians, he was a prisoner in Rome. Apostle Paul is a living example of what he is talking about in the book of Colossians when he says to us, "Christ in us, the hope of glory" (Colossians 1:27, ESV). He had learned through countless difficulties that Jesus Christ was all he needed and that Christ's strength is made perfect in our own weaknesses. With our own strength, we will continue to fall short of the glory of God, but with Jesus Christ in us, we are unbeatable.

In Exodus 33:12–14, Moses said to God,

> One day Moses said to the Lord, "You have been telling me, 'Take these people up to the Promised Land.' But you haven't told me whom you will send with me. You have told me, 'I know you by name, and I look favorably on you.' If it is true that you look favorably on me, let me know your ways so I may understand you more fully and continue to enjoy your favor. And remember that this nation is your very own people."

The Lord replied, "I will personally go with you, Moses, and I will give you rest—everything will be fine for you."

EXODUS 33:12–14 (NLT)

Who will help you? Who will stand with you? Look at what God's answer is to Moses: "My presence will go with you, and I will give you rest." What an assurance that our Father gives us. Because of the Lord's presence with us, we can have rest in the midst of our storms. God wants His people to know that He is in control of their lives. He requires you to desire Him and to take Him into account. He needs to be the priority in your life. He wishes you to trust in Him and in His promises. He wants to make of you a living testimony. Trials should not surprise us or cause us to doubt God's faithfulness. Rather, we should actually be glad to go through them because out of them will spring forth our tenacity, our strong will, our inner man, and our building up to stand. God sends trials to strengthen our trust in Him so that our faith will not fail us. This poem by an unknown author has been a comfort to me in many of my trials. When doubt wants to creep in, remember this:

THE WILL OF GOD

The will of God will never take you,
Where the grace of God cannot keep you.
Where the arms of God cannot support you,
Where the riches of God cannot supply your needs,
Where the power of God cannot endow you.

The will of God will never take you,
Where the spirit of God cannot work through you,
Where the wisdom of God cannot teach you,
Where the army of God cannot protect you,
Where the hands of God cannot mold you.

The will of God will never take you,
Where the love of God cannot enfold you,
Where the mercies of God cannot sustain you,
Where the peace of God cannot calm your fears,
Where the authority of God cannot overrule for you.

The will of God will never take you,
Where the comfort of God cannot dry your tears,
Where the Word of God cannot feed you,
Where the miracles of God cannot be done for you,
Where the omnipresence of God cannot find you.

NEW LEVELS NEW DEVILS

How far do you want to mature in God? Jesus said in the book of John 10:10 (NKJV), "The thief does not come except to steal, and to kill, and to destroy. I have come that they may have life and that they may have it more abundantly." Are you living in the abundance of Christ? Would you like to experience the fullness of God? Then, you must be willing to come up higher. Let me explain: many people fall away from living their lives for Christ because they think that it is a whole lot easier to live for this world than for Christ. They realize that once they accept Jesus Christ as their Savior, their lives become more complicated and more difficult. This is what is turning many people off from living a consecrated life. The thing that you have to remember is that Satan does not need to oppress the people in the world. He is the prince of this world. "Satan, who is the god of this world, has blinded the minds of those who don't believe. They are incapable of perceiving the glorious light of the Good News. They don't comprehend this message about the glory of Christ, who is the exact image of God" (2 Corinthians 4:4, NLT). Since they are not seeking God and God's kingdom, they are not a danger to him. The individuals who are living their lives every day for Christ are a threat to him.

Years ago, I met Joao, and as I tried to share Christ with him and invite him to church, he told me that he was the son of a Brazilian pastor, but he had chosen to stay neutral because he knew that the day he starts to serve Jesus Christ, the devil would not leave him alone, and his life would become more challenging. And he continued to tell me that he had been against his wife giving her life to Christ, but she did, nevertheless. The week that she started attending church was the week that she lost a large sum of money. What do you say to someone who is convinced that they will not be able to fight the good fight of faith and they will be defeated by the devil?

In a nutshell, this is why, as Christians, things seem to get a lot worse before they get better. It is when you are closer to your breakthrough in your spiritual life that you meet the most resistance. Living poor and miserable is an easy, comfortable, and common way to live. When you decide to evict poverty, the battle begins. You do not need to go very far to find depressing and gloomy things and people. They are all around you. Have you ever taken the time to look at the people on the streets? During rush hour? There is an abundance of despair in the world. There is an abundance of misery in the world. Years ago, I heard of a man who was broke and wanted to make some money urgently. He set up a 900-phone line for people to call him if they needed to talk. He was charging by the minute. He indicated that he never estimated so many people to be lonely and in such predicaments just to find somebody to talk to. He ended up shutting down the phone line very quickly because he said he could no longer listen to the unhappiness in the lives of those people. Their depressing state was having an ill effect on him; housewives, husbands, wives, and rich and poor people were willing to pay him just to be able to talk to someone.

Ask yourself if that is what God has in store for you in life. Really. If that were the case, then that would indicate that the Word of God is lacking. The Word of God says that even though you walk through the valley of death, you do not have to fear any evil because He is with you. In His Word, God declares that He intends to keep His promises to us because He can never lie. He is unable to lie. Then, compare this to your reality. How does it hold? If you trust in the Word of God, you will relax knowing that God is on your side, He is for you, and what you are going through is only temporary. It will have a positive outcome any which way you choose to look at it. To be able to look beyond these things and to see the beauty and joy that surround us proves to be very difficult, I have to admit.

I have to tell you that the solution is in the Word

of God. It is called walking by faith. Jesus tells us to walk by faith, not by sight. "For we walk by faith, not by sight" (2 Corinthians 5:7, ESV). It is a powerful concept. You cannot let the carnal things that you see and touch govern your possibilities. For you to experience true joy, happiness, and success, you must learn to walk by faith. Your conditions are guaranteed to always change; nevertheless, be aware that there is a peace that comes to you during a storm or in any episode that you find yourself in when you are able to walk by faith. God has promised to help us if we keep our eyes fixed on Jesus. He promises to draw near to all who draw near to Him. "Come close to God, and God will come close to you" (James 4:8, NLT).

Our God is a remarkable God who promises to rescue us from every storm. He promises to hold us by the hand in Psalm 37:24 (NLT), "Though they stumble, they will never fall, for the LORD holds them by the hand." The enemy attacks us violently when we are trying to invade new territory. Every time that our ministry has planted a church in a different area, we have suffered attacks through the hands of the principalities in that particular area where the church is located. His first means of attack is deception. You need to go beyond allowing discouragement and fear to incapacitate you or whatever weakness his lies may trigger in your existence.

I wonder how many of you reading this book right now are struggling with feelings of discouragement and feeling disconnected. These kinds of attacks will use a very subtle form of deception and will target your weaknesses. As an example, if you are easily discouraged, the attack will be negativity and discouragement concerning your spiritual position, finances, health, relationship, or work situation. These attacks may be triggered by a spirit of heaviness that leaves you feeling isolated, with no stamina, alone, and lonely. They will draw the life out of you, leaving you feeling drained, weary, lethargic, or sleepy. They will cause you to want to give up, do nothing, and be complacent in your walk with God. These attacks are meant to keep you from establishing the kingdom of heaven and being operational in the work of God. This is one of the Bible's explanations of the devil: "You belong to your father, the devil, and you want to carry out your father's desire. He was a murderer from the beginning, not holding on to the truth, for there is no truth in him. When he lies, he speaks his native language, for he is a liar and the father of lies" (John 8:44, NLT). If you are on the brink of a major spiritual breakthrough and you are experiencing these emotions, it is an attack of the enemy to keep you from achieving your divine potential and purpose.

Let me share this with you: "There is therefore now no condemnation for those who are in Christ Jesus" (Romans 8:1, NIV). If you are stressed, anxious, and fearful, be mindful of 2 Timothy 1:7 (NKJV): "For God has not given us a spirit of fear, but of power and of love and of a sound mind."

If you feel lonely, exhausted, gloomy, sad, and desperate, Isaiah 61:1–3:

> The Spirit of the Lord GOD is upon me; because the LORD hath anointed me to preach good tidings unto the meek; he hath sent me to bind up the brokenhearted, to proclaim liberty to the captives, and the opening of the prison to them that are bound; To proclaim the acceptable year of the LORD, and the day of vengeance of our God; to comfort all that mourn; To appoint unto them that mourn in Zion, to give unto them beauty for ashes, the oil of joy for mourning, the garment of praise for the spirit of heaviness; that they might be called trees of righteousness, the planting of the LORD, that he might be glorified.

ISAIAH 61:1–3 (KJV)

If you are being enticed, tempted, searching for an escape through fleshy ways,

But that prophet or that dreamer of dreams shall be put to death, because he has taught rebellion against the Lord your God, who brought you out of the land of Egypt and redeemed you out of the house of slavery, to make you leave the way in which the Lord your God commanded you to walk. So, you shall purge the evil from your midst.

DEUTERONOMY 13:5 (NASB)

Additionally, Proverbs 7:21 (NIV) declares, "With persuasive words she led him astray; she seduced him with her smooth talk." Do not believe every lie of the enemy; I beckon you.

If these outbreaks are leaving you with a lack of inspiration, and you feel withdrawn and complacent and with a lack of stimulus, do not allow the enemy to make you feel defeated.

"The Holy Spirit gives life; the flesh amounts to nothing. The words I have spoken to you—they are full of the Spirit and life. Yet there are some of you who do not believe." For Jesus had known from the beginning which of them did not believe and who would betray him. He went on to say, "This is why I told you that no one can come to me unless the Father has enabled them." From the time He proclaimed this, many of his disciples turned back and no longer followed him.

Jesus asked his twelve disciples, "You do not want to leave too, do you?" Jesus asked the Twelve and Simon Peter answered him, "Lord, to whom we shall go? You have the words of eternal life."

JOHN 6:63–68 (NIV)

I pray for you right now: may these attacks on your life be bound in the name of Jesus. You will make it, and you will accomplish your divine purpose in Jesus's name.

FAITH IT UNTIL YOU MAKE IT

Essentially, this means that you are to keep the faith until the manifestation of God is complete. Now, how many of you find this to be very challenging to do at times? It's hard to stay authentic and trusting, joyful when all in the natural feels so hopeless. But you know what I have learned? Giving up is easy, very easy. Anything worth having entails a fight. Keeping the faith, waiting, and permitting God to work things out requires determination, consistency, and strong will. In the end, you will see God's glory, and you will be compensated.

Keeping the faith sometimes means not knowing what the precise conclusion will be and not having the assurance of a positive outcome, but then again, you are trusting that God's will is greater than your own. As human beings exercising our own free will, we want things when and how we want them, and following someone else's will is hard. We tend to be rebellious, an inheritance from our forefathers who disobeyed God. Surrendering to God is hard to do. We want to tell God how quickly, when, and how He should do it. We stress to God when we make up our own minds that it should be done. We ask so many questions, "O Lord, why do I have to wait so long? Why don't You do it this way? It is quicker. Why don't You use this person? I am ready to see the manifestation." But thank God that "His thoughts are not our thoughts and His ways our ways." God knows what is best for His children. I encourage you today to keep the faith regardless of how hopeless your storm feels to you. Be consistent. God has already worked it out for your good. Faith it until you make it!

Without a doubt, God can do immeasurably more than we can think or imagine. The stronger our faith grows, the greater our determination to prevail will be. You ask, "How can I grow my faith?" As you experience God, as God continues to unfold His plan for your life, as He takes you out of storm after storm, conflict after conflict, as you read God's Word and books like this one, your faith will spring forth, and your trust in your Maker will greatly increase. The Bible says that we have all received a measure of faith, but the responsibility to grow it rests within us. Someone said only God can know the number of apples that will come from an apple seed, but with the eyes of faith, our ability to see is enormous. Surrender your fears to God, learn that storms, obstacles, and problems are God's way and plan for building your faith, learn to depend and trust on God's promises, and persist until you receive your breakthrough. One of the things that I use is P.U.S.H. (pray until something happens). As you go through the storms of life, choose to live daily in the faith sector, not the fear sector, and see what the Lord will be able to accomplish with your faith.

A friend of mine from Haiti once described to me what it feels like to be in a natural storm when you are from the countryside and living in a hut. As the storm approaches, he recalled, the uncertainty of the outcome of the storm and the predictions over the damage expected from that storm suffice to give one human being a bad heart or a heart attack. The predictions stated out loud and in people's minds are, "Will we survive the storms? Will our family members and our young children? Will they survive it?" The violence that hits as the storm rages can send someone afloat and throw them away, never to be seen again. People huddled together, clenched to each other, mothers and fathers holding on to their children, covering them with their bodies, as the strong covers the weak to keep them from flying under the strength. All you hear is voices going up to heaven, singing praises and humming, waiting for the storm to pass. Suddenly, as fast as it came in, it rescinded, and the aftermath as people come out of their hiding places, holes, and underground to look over the damage to figure out who made it and who did not make it; children start dancing on the streets because the storm has regressed. Praises and exclamations of joy are heard because they have made it out of that storm. Some people will be angry at God that He allowed the storm to hit them. As children of God, some storms may violently overtake us and our attitude; our determination during the storm and our conviction determine the outcome. As children of God, what we experience and allow during a storm results in a positive or a negative, and even after the storm, when looking at the aftermath, all we are saying is thank You for that conflict. We should say, "I have come out, and I am more ready for the next step, the next level, the next challenge, the next opportunity."

FAITH AT WORK: LEARNING TO RECOGNIZE YOUR DIVINE HELPERS AND YOUR BLESSINGS

We all need helpers in our lives. To think that anyone can be self-sufficient and require no helpers is to live in self-misconception. You connect with divine helpers through your relationships. A relationship that does not help you as a blessing or to be blessed does not belong in your life. I can tell you that I have been in those types of relationships that were not a blessing to me, that were not adding to my life but subtracting from it. I stayed there too long, thinking that there was a blessing somewhere and that it would come. Don't make that mistake. If the thought keeps coming to your mind and your heart that there is nothing for you in this relationship, nothing to uphold you, nothing to add to your life, chances are, there is not. Move on. God will make the connections and send you your appointed helpers.

Helpers have something you don't have but

desperately require in your life to move you to the next level and fulfill your divine mandate. Your helper will bring revelation, awareness, information, understanding, and insight into your life. Your helpers may not be rich financially but may have information that money cannot purchase. There are many important things that money can never buy. Let's look at the Syrian's servant of Naaman. She was not rich, but she had powerful information about the prophetic ability Elisha possessed. She knew that Elisha could heal her master if only he went before him and humbled himself. If Naaman had rejected the counsel of his servant because she wasn't rich, he would have remained and died a leper.

Your helpers connect you to the people who have what is essential for you; they open doors for you, clear the way before you, empower you, upkeep you, uphold your hand in battle, strengthen you, and build you up when you are weak. Helpers can see what you cannot see because of your circumstances and your closeness to them. The Lord brings such people into your life to bring you clarity, direction, revelation, and accurate counsel that will break the chains that limit and contain you to a particular physical location and to individuals. Helpers come into your life to release you from your limitations and to become all the Lord has intended for you to be.

You need wisdom, humility, and the grace of God to receive the helpers God sends into our lives. It is tough for so many people to just close their mouths, listen to divine counsel through the mouth of a helper, and pray about it. I have encountered people the Lord had assigned me to be a blessing to, but some of them were so arrogant, so full of themselves, and so selfish that they were not able to recognize it. You do not need to try to prove something to your helpers, to show them that "you are all that and a bag of chips," as the saying goes, but you should receive whatever help the Lord has assigned them into your life to give to you.

If you don't treat your helpers with respect and allow them to accomplish their purpose in your life, they will go out of your life without achieving their divine assignment. New helpers will not come into your life when you treat the previous ones poorly. Until you learn to recognize and treat your helpers with respect, they won't be attracted to remain in your life.

No matter how important you are, no matter the level that God has brought you to, you need helpers in your life. Despite how intelligent you are, you need assistants in your life. No matter how successful you are, you need helpers in your life. The Bible says in the book of Revelation Chapter 3:17 (ESV), "For you say, I am rich, I have prospered, and I need nothing, not realizing that you are wretched, pitiable, poor, blind, and naked." It is only a fool who says, "I am rich, and I require nothing." No matter how well you think your life is functioning, you still need your helpers in your life. You need to be humble and gracious and receive them by faith.

To draw helpers into your life, you need to engage yourself in the practice of prayer. There are miracles waiting to happen in your life, and if you are not broken, be humble and learn to combat in the place of prayer. God wants great things to happen in our lives, but nothing happens until we pray. We must pray with fervency and a sense of earnestness. Pray fervently and call forth your helpers wherever they are on this earth, and God will begin to direct them into your path and into your life.

CHAPTER 3:

PUT ON YOUR HIGH PRAISE

The enemy does not like it when we shout hallelujah. Every hallelujah shouted by a believing Christian is a blow to the kingdom of hell. I challenge you to take a praise break right now, throw your arms in the air, and shout hallelujah. Feel the peace of God come over you; feel a hint of joy in your inner being. Every year, our ministry holds a program that we have entitled "Dunamis Nite of Wonders," three (3) magnificent days filled with powerful, anointed praise and worship with powerfully anointed men and women of God. One of the nights is what we call the Dunamis Live Gospel Concert. This concert is an international endeavor with carefully selected gospel artists from around the world coming together in a college auditorium to praise and worship God. The place is usually packed to capacity. We use this time to thank God for all He has done for us and praise and worship Him. It is all about Him in that concert. Testimonies have abounded as people recall the healings, deliverances, and breakthroughs that happened in that concert. People come with their dancing shoes, ready to praise the Lord. And that is what we should be doing all the time, giving thanks and praising our Lord and Savior for who He is.

One night, I had a dream that I had gone to the kingdom of hell to collect all of my belongings that had been stolen by the enemy. As I was leaving, I met with Satan, and as I saw him, I shouted, "Jesus!" and he bowed his head. I tried it again, shouted, "Jesus!" and he bowed his head, and I realized that it was true that when we call on the name of Jesus, the enemy bowed his head. The Word of God says, "Enter His gates with thanksgiving and His courts with praise; give thanks to Him and praise His name" (Psalm 100:4, NIV). The Greek word *Dunamis* is used 120 times in the New Testament. It refers to the "strength, power, or ability of God." It is the root word of our English words "dynamite," "dynamo," and "dynamic."

ATTACK THE ENEMY VIOLENTLY!

"Through You we will push back our adversaries; Through Your name we will trample down those who rise up against us" (Psalm 44:5, NASB). There is healing, power, and deliverance in the name of Jesus.

Have you read the book of Nehemiah in the Bible? This book of Nehemiah tends not to be very popular, but it is an amazing story of how to deal with the enemies of your soul, and if understood well, it will equip you for life's battles until the day that God calls you home. The book of Nehemiah is designed to teach us that only with God's help can we receive victory from our enemies. Only with God's help can we change ourselves and recover from any attack or storm in our lives. The story of Nehemiah is about rebuilding the walls. Ordinarily, in life, a wall symbolizes strength and protection. In ancient times, the only means of defense against the enemies was a wall. Sometimes, these walls were tremendously thick and tall. The book of Daniel recalls that the walls surrounding Babylon were about 380 feet thick and 100 feet high. You can imagine, but how does that relate to you and me today? The rebuilding of the walls means re-establishing your strength. Sometimes, when people are going through storms, their defenses in a moment of weakness crumble away. Depending on the storm, they might feel helpless and hopeless. If this is you, if this is the way that you are feeling right now, take comfort in knowing that the walls of your life can be rebuilt with strength, power, and purpose again.

In Nehemiah Chapter 4, we read:

> Sanballat was very angry when he learned that we were rebuilding the wall. He flew into a rage and mocked the Jews saying in front of his friends and the Samarian army officers, "What does this bunch of poor, feeble Jews think they're doing? Do they think they can build the wall in a single day by just offering a few sacrifices? Do they actually think they can make something of stones from a rubbish heap—and charred ones at that?" In trying to rebuild your walls, in trying to regain your strength, your enemies will be angry at you.
>
> Tobiah the Ammonite, who was standing beside him, remarked, "That stone wall would collapse if even a fox walked along the top of it!" Then I prayed, "Hear us, our God, for we are being mocked. May their scoffing fall back on their own heads and may they themselves become captives in a foreign land! Do not ignore their guilt. Do not blot out their sins, for they have provoked you to anger here in front of the builders." Some people may mock you, ridicule you but keep on pressing. It will come into place.

At last the wall was completed to half its height around the entire city, for the people had worked with enthusiasm. But when Sanballat and Tobiah and the Arabs, Ammonites, and Ashdodites heard that the work was going ahead and that the gaps in the wall of Jerusalem were being repaired, they were furious. They all made plans to come and fight against Jerusalem and throw us into confusion. The enemies would not want to believe that you are evading and might intensify the attacks to intimidate you, to frighten you into staying in bondage. But we prayed to our God and guarded the city day and night to protect ourselves.

Then the people of Judah began to complain, "The workers are getting tired, and there is so much rubble to be moved. We will never be able to build the wall by ourselves." You are strong because of what God has deposited inside of you. Meanwhile, our enemies were saying, "Before they know what's happening, we will swoop down on them and kill them and end their work."

NEHEMIAH 4:1–11 (NLT)

This is always the plan of the enemy for you: attack you while you are not paying attention. When you stop praying, you start playing. The Word of God tells us to pray without ceasing (1 Thessalonians 5:17).

The Jews who lived near the enemy came and told us again and again, "They will come from all directions and attack us!" So I placed armed guards behind the lowest parts of the wall in the exposed areas. I stationed the people to stand guard by families, armed with swords, spears, and bows." Your prayer warriors, your intercessors will come in handy at the time of battle.

Then as I looked over the situation, I called together the nobles and the rest of the people and said to them, "Don't be afraid of the enemy! Remember the Lord, who is great and glorious, and fight for your brothers, your sons, your daughters, your wives, and your homes!" God who is a fighter, who is your divine covering, your protector will always provide and protect you in any combat.

When our enemies heard that we knew of their plans and that God had frustrated them, we all returned to our work on the wall. But from then on, only half my men worked while the other half stood guard with spears, shields, bows, and coats of mail. The leaders stationed themselves behind the people of Judah who were building the wall. The laborers carried on their work with one hand supporting their load and one hand holding a weapon. All the builders had a sword belted to their side. The trumpeter stayed with me to sound the alarm.

Then I explained to the nobles and officials and all the people, "The work is very spread out, and we are widely separated from each other along the wall. When you hear the blast of the trumpet, rush to wherever it is sounding. Then our God will fight for us!"

We worked early and late, from sunrise to sunset.

And half the men were always on guard. I also told everyone living outside the walls to stay in Jerusalem. That way they and their servants could help with guard duty at night and work during the day. During this time, none of us—not I, nor my relatives, nor my servants, nor the guards who were with me—ever took off our clothes. We carried our weapons with us at all times, even when we went for water.

NEHEMIAH 4:12–23 (NLT)

You can never abandon your weapons. We know, according to 2 Corinthians 10:4 (KJV), that "For the weapons of our warfare are not carnal, but mighty through God to the pulling down of strongholds."

You will not be able to build the walls of your life if you are not greatly concerned about the impact that your storm is having on your being. When you are going through a storm, do you take the time to assess where you are and where God wants to take you? Again, I say if you are going through a storm of correction, confess and take the necessary steps to correct that which is not of God. If not a storm of correction, know that God is taking you somewhere. He has a plan and a divine purpose for your existence. By the way, did I tell you to always let the Holy Spirit guide you and give you understanding as you read God's Word? Some of your unfriendly friends might try to discourage you, thinking that you are too far gone to come back.

I met a woman at some point in my ministry. She had been a high-class prostitute. Her mother was a prostitute and had been convicted of the death of her father. She was born while her mother was in jail, serving her sentence for the death of her father. She had traveled from state to state practicing prostitution, then settled in Las Vegas under the authority of a pimp. She had many children, but they were all taken away from her. One daughter had been given to her mother when she came out of jail, two of her sons were taken by her sister, and two were adopted, and she did not know where they were. She had been mugged, beaten, cut in her face, robbed at knifepoint, and jailed before she came to Christ. She changed her life, quit prostitution, and moved to a different state to start afresh. She gave birth to two sons and was trying to the best of her ability to make a new life for herself and her children. Her own family, church family, and friends would not lend her a hand and would not accept her because they did not think that she would make it. The same people who were praying for her deliverance from drug addiction and prostitution turned against her. They could not appreciate the work of God in her life.

By all odds, her family thought that she would not make it back, but today, she is a Christian. She has rebuilt her life. Does she still struggle? Yes, but then she has learned to rely on Jesus.

We recognize that the flesh that exists in us resists the things, the methods, the work, and the will of God. You must know that whenever you are going through a storm, when you decide to rise above your storm, the enemy makes the decision to increase his opposition. You are not dealing with an enemy who is untested. You are dealing with an enemy that has many decades of experience and who is subtle and unscrupulous but who can never be stronger than God. Satan causes things to become problematic when we decide to start fighting and believe the Word of God. The enemy can surely wear you out; nonetheless, he cannot wear you down.

Identify that when in a storm, prayer should be your first response, not your last resort. Have you ever heard about the first responders? Our first responder is the Word of God and praying according to His Word. God wants us to rely on Him when we are going through storms; we do this by praying.

In times of conflict, request God to battle your enemies for you. Learn to depend on God. Do not be distracted. Turn your enemies into the hands of God. He is a just God. Allow God to deal with them. Remember, the enemies want to make you feel defeated, discouraged, passive, or inward-focused. Moreover, the enemy rages against any progress that we make in God. The attacks of the enemy may intensify as you become stronger spiritually. As we see in the story of Nehemiah, as they resisted and continued to build the wall, the enemies planned a bigger attack to demoralize them completely. As the work progressed, the enemy became more serious. They threatened and planned more violent attacks.

Notice that it would have been easier for the people to give in to their fear and stop. And as you can see, the enemies did not really attack; they just threatened. The same is true with you. If you give in when the enemy is threatening you, you might miss the mark. Hold on! I told you that Satan still uses this same strategy of fear to threaten us, and if you fall under the fear of what might be, then you have lost. My prayer for you is that you will be strengthened by the reading of this book, and by applying the biblical principles described here, you will win over your fear and always come out on top. God is your refuge and strength. The Bible says in Isaiah 54:17 (NKJV), "'No weapon formed against you shall prosper, and every tongue which rises against you in judgment you shall condemn. This is the heritage of the servants of the Lord, and their righteousness is from Me,' says the Lord." I want to encourage you by letting you know that you can live a life without chains. And how do you do that? By discovering that your most important defense is to recognize the enemy and know how to defeat it. Remember, you cannot rectify what you have not identified.

You might be tempted to become worried and let the tactics of the enemy terrify you. You might be tempted to give up, to stop praying, and to become a spectator in your own life. Resolve to have a mind to work, resolve to travail before the Throne of Grace, and stand against everything that the enemy represents and keep holding on. You will make it, and your enemy will be defeated. Your victory was won at the cross.

I must warn you that sometimes people make the mistake of trying to hold on to a temporary helper, causing chaos in their lives. So many people have married and gotten involved in a lasting relationship with someone the Lord had sent as a helper to allow them to reach the next level. Be in prayer in asking God to give discernment and wisdom in not only identifying your helpers but also in differentiating the temporary helpers from the permanent helpers. Be blessed.

HUM A SONG OF PRAISE

Hum a song of praise. That is all there is to it. Through our storms, our trials, and our tribulations, we arrive at that place where we learn to trust in Jesus and to rely on His Word. His Word is unchangeable. John 10:10 (KJV) says, "The thief comes only to steal and kill and destroy; I have come that they may have life and have it to the full." Just reading this verse brings a smile to my face. Jesus said to you and me that He has come so that we could have life and have it in abundance. That means that not only will you inherit eternal life, but you and I should be living a life that is abundant. I heard a preacher say, "Nothing broken, nothing lacking, nothing missing; this is the abundance of God." And when we come to Christ, this is the promise He makes to us. Matthew 6:33 (ESV) states, "But seek first his kingdom and his righteousness, and all these things will be given to you as well." Aren't you glad you belong to Jesus and not the world?

Many people believe that they should only praise God after they have received an answer to a prayer or after God has done something for them. Some think that it is optional, and some only praise and thank God when circumstances in their lives are good. Once situations change and things are not going well, they stop praising and thanking God. The truth of the matter is that praising God is not elective. Praise has a very highly effective outcome on you, God, and the devil. In Hebrews 1:19 (ESV), we read, "You have loved righteousness and hated wickedness; therefore God, your God, has anointed you with the oil of gladness beyond your companions."

How does praise affect you? When you burst in praise to God, you are acknowledging that it is not your own efforts that bring the blessings. By keeping focus on your storm, you might become bitter, self-centered, and even prideful. Praise has a way of getting you to focus on God and taking your attention away from your problems. Some people try to pray, but their minds are so focused on the problem at hand that they complain more than they pray. A better way to keep from complaining and focusing on your problems, your debts, lack of money, and others is to praise. If you feel that you cannot get yourself in an attitude of praise, hum a praise song. As you do so, things will change, and you will find yourself deep in praying and praising. Lift your hands and just start telling God how thankful you are for all He has done for you. There is a hymn with powerful words that states, "Count God's blessings in your life, analyze them, / then you will see in worship the abundance of blessings in your life."

Acquire some powerful, anointed praise CDs, play them around your house, and you will see the atmosphere change. The feeling of heaviness will be lifted, and the joy of the Lord will replace it. The most important thing that you can do is praise God. A negative attitude will not change overnight, but beginning the process of praising God will also begin the transformation in your attitude. Philippians 4:4 (NET) states, "Rejoice in the Lord always: and again, I say, Rejoice." When you begin prayer with praise and end with praise, you build yourself up spiritually. You strengthen yourself in the Lord. Philippians 4:6–7 (NIV) states, "Do not be anxious about anything, but in every situation, by prayer and petition, with thanksgiving, present your requests to God. And the peace of God, which transcends all understanding, will guard your hearts and your minds in Christ Jesus."

Apostle Paul put it all in perspective for us in 2 Corinthians 4:17–18 (NIV) when he said, "For our light and momentary troubles are achieving for us an eternal glory that far outweighs them all. So we fix our eyes not on what is seen, but on what is unseen, since what is seen is temporary, but what is unseen is eternal." Notice that he says our afflictions are momentary, just for a moment, compared to our eternal life. You heard of the story of Paul and Silas when they were thrown in jail. In shackles, they busted in praise for the Lord. It was their praise that released the power of God and the earthquake that opened the doors and delivered them from their jail. Praise must be our foundation. Praise must be a way of life, our lifestyle in Christ, the lifestyle of every believer in Christ.

Praising God is also a powerful weapon against the enemy. Nehemiah 8:10 tells us that praise is strength. Nehemiah said, "Go and enjoy choice food and sweet drinks, and send some to those who have nothing prepared. This day is holy to our Lord. Do not grieve, for the joy of the Lord is your strength" (Nehemiah 8:10, NIV). The enemy wants to steal your joy. In 2 Chronicles 20, Jehoshaphat appointed singers to lead his army into battle with praise unto the Lord. When they went into battle singing and praising God, the Lord set an ambush, and their enemies were defeated. Praise defeats Satan. Praise is giving of yourself to God. God desires to fellowship with us. He is God all by Himself, but there are many instances in the Bible where we are given directives to praise God and the effects of praising Him. Psalm 100:4 (NIV) says, "Enter his gates with thanksgiving and his courts with praise; give thanks to him and praise his name." Andrew Murray, a great man of prayer, said that before he prayed, he often said, "Lord, melt my cold heart, break my hard heart, and prepare it for Your touch." When we go to our Father with such a heart, the Holy Spirit will meet us as our prayer partner and helper, enabling us to approach the Throne of Grace and touch the very heart of God. For God's promise to us still stands in James 4:8 (NKJV), "Draw near to God, and he will draw near to you." God wants to fellowship with you, and praise allows you to enter this fellowship with your Heavenly Father, being in communion with Him, experiencing His intimacy, and getting answers.

SURROUND YOURSELF WITH
PRAYER WARRIORS!

It is important to surround yourself with God's people, an army of prayer warriors to travail on your behalf, bringing your petitions before the Throne of Grace. The Bible says in the book of Matthew 18:19 (KJV), "Again I say to you that if two of you agree on earth concerning anything that they ask, it will be done for them by My Father in heaven." There is power in a prayer of agreement. Notice that I stated prayer warriors, not prayer worriers. There are some people in the church or around you who are prayer worriers. That is not the kind I am talking about. You could be thinking that you do not want to burden your friends with your prayer requests, but a prayer warrior or a true Christian friend will be anxious to pray for you. Make sure to keep them informed of the progress and the situation so that they will know how to intercede for you. You will draw strength from them, and you will be surprised to see the power that emanates from such an army of prayer warriors. The prayer warriors will guard you in prayer. Prayers made on your behalf will bless you. Prayer warriors stick together. They are on the front line of spiritual warfare, and they know how to battle. Those who have been on the front line are better equipped to help those who are heading to the front line. Get encouraged by James 5:16 (NLT): "The earnest prayer of a righteous person has great power and produces wonderful results." I heard T. D. Jakes, who is a long-time pastor of a megachurch, say, "You don't even have to be the one praying, but if you get around somebody who really knows how to pray, prayer will lift you when you've fallen, prayer will catch you when you've lost your grip, prayer will stop you from going overboard, prayer will bring you out!" Prayer warriors can give your prayers more depth. They can see things that you may not be able to see and pray against any supplemental attacks. They are an encouragement to you and can add biblical knowledge to their prayer. They can pray the Scriptures, and they can keep their prayers on track, aiming at each target. They can help you to avoid pitfalls and fiery arrows of the enemy. Make sure that the prayer warriors you entrust your requests to are firmly rooted in the Word of God and God's biblical teachings.

CHAPTER 4:

COMMAND THE DEVIL

Words are powerful. With words, you can construct or destroy. Words can give life or bring death. The power of words goes beyond mankind. God spoke, and the heavens came into being. At God's words, we came into existence. God's words are so powerful, and we are also warned about the power of our words. They have the power to curse or bless. They carry defeat or victory. What words do you speak? Words of life or words of death?

Words are so powerful. They can make or break. Words are powerful. They communicate. They express feelings. They deliver information. They inspire others. They give guidance. They teach. Mere words can allow you to discover someone's feelings and allow people to share their feelings and their plans. Words are declarative. The Bible makes us know that life and death are in the power of the tongue. Let me take you to the beginning.

> In the beginning God said, "Let us make man in our image, in our likeness, and let them rule over the fish of the sea and the birds of the air, over the livestock, over all the earth, and over all the creatures that move along the ground." So, God created man in his own image, in the image of God he created him; male and female he created them.

GENESIS 1:26–27 (ESV)

Then, God created man and breathed life into him. The moment that God breathed His life into man, man was able to speak. Our speech is one of the things that separate us from the animals. When you read the book of Genesis, you notice that man's first job was to name the animals, which required man to speak. Our words are powerful because they are spiritual forces. Our words are not sound waves. We read in the book of John 6:63 (NKJV), "It is the Spirit who gives life; the flesh profits nothing. The words that I speak to you are spirit, and they are life." Let me explain a little further. In John 4:24, Jesus said, "God is Spirit." Since man is created in the image of God, man is also a spirit. Man can act like God in the image of which man is created. "How does God act?" I ask you. God spoke the universe into existence. Repeatedly in the book of Genesis, we read, "And God said." God created everything by speaking it into existence. Hebrews 11:3 (AMPC) states, "By faith we understand that the worlds were framed by the word of God, so that the things which are seen were not made of things which are visible." We understand from that scripture that words, God's words, created the world. God said it, and that settled it. God spoke it, and it came to be.

It is important for you to come to the realization that you can create what you need in your life, the lives of your children, by your words. Solomon said in the book of Proverbs, "Death and life are in the power of the tongue: and they that love it shall eat the fruit thereof" (Proverbs 18:21, ESV). Man's word can produce great power. As a child of God, your words are even more powerful. You can command the devil; you can command great blessings into your life. The book of Job says in the 22nd chapter, verse 28, "You will also decree a thing, and it will be established for you; and light will shine on your ways" (Job 22:28, NKJV). Many worldly religions have tried to copy what the Word says. Some have said if you keep saying positive things, then you will see positive things happen in your life and so forth. We know that God has given us the power to speak things into existence by faith and trust in the Word and the promises of God. You are not a weak link but a powerful being with divine authority to speak and command the enemy to take his hands off you, your family, and whatever else that the enemy is messing up with in your life, whether it'd be your children, your finances, your sanity, your thoughts, or your life. Words can be weapons of mass destruction or weapons of mass construction in the mouth of a believer.

CAPTURE YOUR FEAR AND MAKE IT A PRISONER!

Fear is such a strong emotion. Have you ever looked at it that way? Whatever you are afraid of is very real to you. I told you in the previous chapters about my fear of snakes and how it paralyzed my life for years. I was able to overcome that fear when God showed me that what I was afraid of was what I imagined to be something bigger than me. I understand fear; I do not take it lightly when someone tells me that they are afraid of something. You have to know that fear is a powerful destructive weapon of the enemy. He uses fear as a way to keep you in bondage, in ignorance, and in shackles. No matter the fear, it creates a paralysis in your life. Nowadays, people have developed many types of phobias, and millions of money are being spent on therapy to help people overcome and get a grip on their fear. I knew a woman who was afraid of taking the elevator. Her life was so limited because she would not go anywhere that she could not get through the stairs. There was only a limited flight of stairs that she could go up to. She was missing so much out of life. She could not visit certain places. She could not go to certain restaurants and so many other things because she was afraid of being in an elevator.

What about you? What is your fear? I know another woman who became afraid of her children as they grew older. She became afraid to discipline them; she became afraid to raise her voice at them. What is your fear? What are you afraid of? Some people are afraid of success, some are afraid of rejection, and some are afraid of demons. Is anything keeping you in chains today? Then, it is time to face that fear and come out on top. The Word of God states, "For God has not given us a spirit of fear and timidity, but of power, love, and self-discipline" (2 Timothy

1:17, NLT). Fear is the single most destructive force warring against us. I remember that I was invited to preach at a conference in Miami, Florida. The conference was to last from Sunday to Sunday, and each night, one specific speaker would speak. It was my first time speaking in that type of setting. On the last day of the conference, all the guest preachers who had spoken during the week would all speak. I was the only female preacher there. Speaking to a group of 350 people as the only female Black preacher was okay, but on that last Sunday evening, when we were all scheduled to share, fear totally gripped me. As we sat in the pastor's office before joining the congregation, I looked around, and I suddenly became so aware that I was the only woman pastor there. Actually, I was the only pastor there. Across from me were bishops and apostles. I felt so small compared to them. When I looked at the lineup for the night, I would be the last one to share. Panic and I became one. I wondered how I would follow all those great men of God.

I don't remember much of the beginning of the service. I was too busy being afraid and apprehensive. I was praying and sweating. Would I remember what I wanted to speak about? Would I be able to walk and not stumble? All manner of scary, awful thoughts were coming to my mind. That fear meant to strip me of power and cause me to completely lose control. I finally, with much prayer, was able to stand up and deliver one of the best messages that I have ever preached. The presence of God was so strong that night. People were healed and delivered.

At the end of the service, one apostle who had traveled from Nigeria to attend the program told me that he did not even want me to stop preaching because I seemed to be so connected to God, and revelations were coming out of my mouth so deeply that he just wanted to sit and listen. This was one of the people whom I feared the most to follow. The fear meant for me not to deliver. I was afraid of a picture that my imagination had painted for me, an image so vivid that it looked to be real to me. It was not based on the truth but on a false assumption. That is fear. Fear finds its basis in certain assumptions so strong that you believe that they are the truth, and they take the place of reality in your mind. Fear wants to rob us of our identity in Christ. Let me remind you of this. Instead of a spirit of fear, God has bestowed upon us a Spirit of power, love, and self-control; God gave us authority. You have to change your mindset and replace these assumptions with the real truth. It is a process. Jesus Christ is the truth. Do you want to rid yourself of every fear, fear of the unknown, fear of the enemy, fear of people? Look to Jesus, who is our truth; take time to replace every lie and every assumption with the truth. Jesus told him, "I am the way, the truth, and the life" (John 14:6, NIV).

The title of this segment is to capture your fear and make it a prisoner. Discover your identity in Christ and let the Holy Spirit dismantle every lie that the enemy has made you believe. God created you. Remember that fear is not from God. Every time you feel fear, just know that it is a manifestation of the kingdom of darkness. The devil uses fear to keep God's children in bondage and prevent them from coming into complete communion with Jesus Christ. Is fear stopping you? Are you afraid of something tangible? Maybe you fear failure, change, success, or something else that is more difficult to pin down. No matter what is scaring you, learn to acknowledge, confront, and take control of your fear in order to overcome it through the Word of God. Fear can only bring torment.

"There is no fear in love; but perfect love casts out fear, because fear involves torment. But he who fears has not been made perfect in love" (1 John 4:18, NIV). All of us must learn to face our fears. David said in Psalm 56:3 (NIV), "Whenever I am afraid, I will trust in You." I looked up the type of fears out there at the library, and there were over four pages of known fears or phobias. Another thing it also included was phobophobia, which is the fear of being afraid. The list is extensive. Many times, in the Word, God encourages us not to fear.

Isaiah 41:10 (NKJV) says, "Fear not, for I am with you; be not dismayed, for I am your God. I will strengthen you, yes, I will help you, I will uphold you with My righteous right hand." Our Father works with us to bring us out of every bondage and into liberty. If you have been afraid of something and desire to be free, the time will come when you have to face your fear. It would be easy to deny or ignore your fears in a society that is stressful and gloating about courage. I heard it say that courage is not the absence of fear, but it is to acknowledge your fear and take action in spite of your fear. By owning your feelings today by acknowledging them, you have taken the first step toward that liberty promised to us by our Lord. In addition, sometimes fear makes itself known, and at other times, it is more difficult to name those anxious feelings lurking in the back of your mind. I promise you if you take Jesus's hand, you can be certain that He is with you and will help you face your fears. I cannot say it enough: you cannot rectify what you have not identified and what you are refusing to face. Your freedom will manifest in Jesus's name.

THE DEVIL IS NOT YOUR FRIEND; HE IS YOUR ENEMY

The dictionary describes an enemy as someone who hates another, someone who attacks or tries to harm another, someone or something that harms or threatens someone, one that is antagonistic to another, especially one seeking to injure, overthrow, or confound an opponent, something harmful or deadly, a hostile unit or force.

As previously stated, the Bible has identified for us in John 10:10 who the enemy is. God has revealed to us in His Word who the devil is and what he represents. This verse exposes him, his goals, and his desires. The only reason the thief ever shows up is to steal, kill, and destroy. The word "steal" means that he is trying to take something from you. First Peter 5:8 (KJV) states, "Be sober, be vigilant; because your adversary the devil, as a roaring lion, walketh about, seeking whom he may devour." Now, the devil never comes to you looking like a thief or a roaring lion. He is a liar. He comes to you disguised, wanting you to believe that he can be a source of supply for your needs. God is our source of supply. He promised to supply all of your needs. I want you to be careful and not be deceived. The devil is never there for your own benefit. Jesus shared with us that we should not fall for the devices of the enemy, and we cannot serve two (2) masters. "No one can serve two masters; for either he will hate the one and love the other, or else he will be loyal to the one and despise the other. You cannot serve God and mammon" (Matthew 6:24, ESV). Many people have fallen for the false promises of the devil and have deeply regretted it when they realized that they had fallen for his lies and disguises. Satan's agents are not like we see them in movies with the pitchfork in their hands. They are people like you and me; they make you laugh, they joke with you, and they are the people who send you friend requests on Facebook. They are on all the social media sites. They invade your life, and at that point, they start their plan of destroying your life through their manipulations.

One woman I prayed with recounted her story

to me. When she came to me for prayers, she was running away from a deadly relationship. She was being tormented by nightmares to the point that she was afraid to go to sleep. She desperately needed deliverance. She told her story like this: She opened her Facebook account, and like many of you, she was desperate to enlarge her pool of friends and the people she could reach on Facebook. She was accepting friend requests from even any stranger who would send them to her. She accepted a friend request from a man, and soon, he started sending her messages. She responded, and they started a friendship on Facebook. According to her, even though they had not seen each other face to face, they developed an attraction to each other, which advanced into their exchanging phone numbers over a period of time. Although they had not arranged to see each other, they knew it would happen, and they were talking on the phone every day. One late night, as they were lovingly having one of their regular phone conversations, the man shared with her that he was so in love with her that he gave her body, soul, and mind and insisted that she did the same. She was a little bit apprehensive at first, but the man worked through her objections and forced her to repeat the same. As soon as she did, he told her that he was a disciple of Lucifer, that he had met Satan personally, and from the entire time, his goal had been to get her to say that she gave him her soul. This started a long list of satanic manipulation, destruction, intercession, and finally, deliverance in the life of that young woman. The Word of God warns us that Satan can disguise himself as an angel of light. "But I am not surprised! Even Satan disguises himself as an angel of light" (2 Corinthians 11:14, NLT).

I have met plenty of witches in my line of work. One comes to mind because she was very cunning and would always do her best to make you believe that she had your best interests at heart. Her goal was to get you in so deep that you would never be able to get out. By the way she spoke, she made her victims trust what she was saying. She made her victims feel like she was on their side and that her goal was to help them against the big bad wolf that wanted to devour them. By the time her victims realized that she had pushed them deeply into the hands of the devil and that she made sure that they couldn't find ways or help to get out, it was very late. One lady testified to me that she had gone to visit this witch with a friend. She only accompanied her friend because the friend was apprehensive about going to a witch's house by herself. She reported that from the time she left that witch's house, she felt something hit her car, and whatever it was started following her. She went back to the witch to report what was happening, and the witch said that she needed to check for her with the spirits and she needed to pay her to do that, which she did. From there, the witch told her that she was on this earth without any spiritual knowledge; she did not know anything about the spiritual realm, and that was a shame. She assured Jeanne that all she wanted to do was to help her and acted toward her like a mother wanting to help a daughter. Pretty quickly, Jeanne started sensing that there were people watching her, following her. Her dreams became troubled. She would have nightmares and started seeing demons in her dreams. When she went to confront the witch, she said that some people would be too happy to serve demons and that she had already introduced Jeanne to so many demons, and they were all following her and stuck to her. When Jeanne told her that she did not understand and she never wanted to serve demons, she told her that the demons liked her and wanted to marry her, that she was chosen to be a witch, and that the witch had already started the process for her. Surprise! The devil never comes to you looking like the devil because you would run away from him, but he always uses camouflage. You need discernment to uncover the plans of the enemy. But glory to God that He can, and He will deliver us.

"Surely, thus says the LORD, 'Even the captives of the mighty man will be taken away, And the prey of the tyrant will be rescued; For I will contend with the one who contends with you'" (Isaiah 49:25, NASB).

Throughout my years in ministry, I have heard so many testimonies and stories about how innocent, honest, and naive people were taken in by witches with the sweetness, compassion, and understanding they seemed to offer them at the beginning, except to find themselves deeply involved in darkness and witchcraft at the end. Women have shared how they fell in love with men who look to be charismatic, nice, and jovial, only to find themselves initiated into demonic affairs, having to fight and rely deeply on God for their freedom and deliverance from this bondage.

Satan is referred to by many names in both the Old and the New Testament. Each name gives a picture of who he is. Abaddon, which means destruction (Revelation 9:11), Accuser (Revelation 12:10), Adversary (1 Peter 5:8), Angel of light (2

Corinthians 11:14), Angel of the bottomless pit (Revelation 9:11), Anointed Covering Cherub (Ezekiel 28:14), Antichrist (1 John 4:8), Apollyon (Revelation 9:11), Beast (Revelation 14:9-10), Beelzebub (Matthew 12:24), Belial (2 Corinthians 6:15), Deceiver (Revelation 12:9), Devil (1 John 3:8), Dragon (Revelation 12:9), Enemy (Matthew 13:39), Evil One (John 17:15), Father of Lies (John 8:4–40), God of this age (2 Corinthians 4:4), King of Babylon (Isaiah 14:4), King of the bottomless pit (Revelation 9:11), King of Tyre (Ezekiel 28:12), Lawless One (2 Thessalonians 2:8–10), Leviathan (Isaiah 27:1), Liar (John 8:44), Little Horn (Daniel 8:9–11), Lucifer (Isaiah 14:12–14), Man of sin (2 Thessalonians 2:2–4), Murderer (John 8:44), Power of Darkness (Colossians 1:13–14) Prince of the power of the air (Ephesians 2:1–2), Roaring lion (1 Peter 5:8), Ruler of the darkness (Ephesians 6:12), Ruler of demons (Luke 11:15), Ruler of this world (John 12:31–32), Satan (Mark 1:13), Serpent of old (Revelation 12:9), Son of perdition (2 Thessalonians 2:3–4), Star (Revelation 9:1), Tempter (Matthew 4:3), Thief (John 10:10), and Wicked One (Ephesians 6:16).

You can see that God has given us an extensive understanding of who the devil is and what he is all about. He is not our friend and is our eternal enemy, and as such, we cannot allow ourselves to play and take him lightly. As you pray, know that however powerful the enemy might be, He who is in us is greater than he who is in the world. There are ministering angels sent to help us according to Hebrews 1:14 (NIV), "Are not all angels ministering spirits sent to serve those who will inherit salvation?" Trust God to lead you in every decision; trust God to save you, deliver you, and guide you.

If you have never heard of the story of Elisha in the Old Testament, I encourage you to take the time and go through it as you are in your storm. Second Kings 6:15–17 states,

> Now when the attendant of the man of God had risen early and gone out, behold, an army with horses and chariots was circling the city. And his servant said to him, "Alas, my master! What shall we do?" So he answered, "Do not fear, for those who are with us are more than those who are with them." Then Elisha prayed and said, "O LORD, I pray, open his eyes that he may see." And the LORD opened the servant's eyes and he saw; and behold, the mountain was full of horses and chariots of fire all around Elisha.

2 KINGS 6:15–17 (NASB)

It does not matter where the enemy has cornered you; just remember that those who are with you are more than those with your enemies. Your victory is assured in Christ Jesus.

MONITOR YOUR INNER CONVERSATION

Apostle Paul prayed in the book of Ephesians 3:16 (NIV), "I pray that out of his glorious riches he may strengthen you with power through his Spirit in your inner being." Our mind can be our most detrimental enemy. What we say to ourselves and what we rehash in our thoughts can take us on the road of destruction and depression. Speak life into yourself. As we go through our storms, we need to watch carefully not only the words that come out of our mouths but also our inner conversations. The most important are these things that you say to yourself. One pastor started a fast one day about certain phrases that we needed to never let come out of our mouths or think because these thoughts would not help us attain victory. Our inner conversations need to be strong, abounding in faith, bold, and certain of the victory in Jesus Christ. Monitoring your inner conversation is crucial while you go through a storm. The Bible says that we need to guard our hearts, guard our souls, and not let any doubt of the enemy enter. There is a verse that I always try to remember about the little foxes in the book of Solomon 2:15 (BSB), "Catch for us the foxes, the little foxes that ruin the vineyards, our vineyards that are in bloom."

One commentary explains it: "Let the blossoming love of the soul be without injury and restraint. Let the rising faith and affection be carefully guarded. Both individuals and communities do well to think of the little foxes that spoil the vines." Watch out for the detrimental thoughts that enter your soul and want to take control and permeate your being with negativity; these thoughts, when you hold on to them, can create a lot of damage. God wants you to live in the light, not in darkness, but our thoughts sometimes want to take us where we do not want to go. One thing that is important is to keep our thoughts under captivity and control what we think. When negativity wants to spoil your inner being, rebuke it and commit yourself not to dwell on it. The Bible says in the book of 2 Corinthians 10:5 (NIV), "We demolish arguments and every pretension that sets itself up against the knowledge of God, and we take captive every thought to make it obedient to Christ."

Monitor your inner conversation and persist in aligning it with God's Word. Learn to take control of your thought life. Believe me, it is not easy to monitor your inner conversation and keep it captive. At any given moment, if you pay attention to yourself, you can detect that your old way of thinking wants to dominate your new way of thinking. The Holy Spirit might be trying to tell you something, and the enemy might also be trying to direct your thought process toward defeat. Hearken to the voice of the Holy Spirit. Rehash what your thoughts were on a given day and compare them to what the Bible says.

Pay close attention to your inner being. It starts from inside. Philippians 4:8 (NIV) says, "Finally, brothers and sisters, whatever is true, whatever is noble, whatever is right, whatever is pure, whatever is lovely, whatever is admirable—if anything is excellent or praiseworthy—think about such things." Practice makes perfect, right? Your actions, reactions, and even the way you treat people at a certain time and place are tied to your inner conversation. You are important; your thoughts are important factors in your life. From your inner being... I promise you if you challenge your inner conversations with scriptures and the truth, you will notice a sizable change in your life. "But the things that come out of a person's mouth come from the heart, and these defile them. For out of the heart come evil thoughts; murder, adultery, sexual immorality, theft, false testimony, slander" (Matthew 15:18–19, NIV). Nurture your spirit with worship, praise, and prayer. Strengthen your inner being with the help of the Holy Spirit, our Helper, our Comforter. Jessy Dixon says, "The Holy Spirit made a promise, / His power will descend, / from your inner being / there will be a river with no end."

HAVE GUT-PUNCHING PHRASES

I encourage you to no longer speak words of defeat about yourself, about your life, about your storm. When you are going through your storm, you need gut-punching phrases guaranteed to motivate, inspire you, and make you see things in a victorious light. Okay. The Bible says in Proverbs 18:21 (NLT), "The tongue can bring death or life; those who love to talk will reap the consequences." You can speak life or death. You can speak victory or defeat, success or failure. It is easier to speak ourselves into defeat than victory, especially when we are going through a storm through challenges. God has deposited strength inside of us, principles to strengthen us in his Word. God is our source, and the Bible is our resource. Deposits for all that we ever need to strengthen us are in the Word of God.

No matter the situation, the problem, the rejection, the humiliation, the pain, and the tribulations, your exit is already in the Word of God. You just need to discover it. This Book has provided you with nuggets of information to show you the way to victory, to overcome, and to experience life in abundance. The enemy will try every possible distraction to keep you from finding out these truths, but keep persisting, keep keeping on, do not ever give up, and you will see the light at the end of the tunnel. The enemy does not want you to speak life to yourself; he wants to isolate you and have his way with you. Stand up right now, shake anything off of you, take some steps forward, and keep on stepping. Your victory is imminent. You will never be defeated. If you are defeated, then Jesus would have sacrificed Himself in vain. Child of God, God sent His only begotten Son for your victory. His blood has washed you clean; do not let your mind tell you otherwise. Rebuke yourself and get up. If you live in an apartment infested with roaches or mice, you do not have food to feed your children. The house is too small, you do not yet have the money to leave, and you do not even know where the money will come from to pay for another apartment; if you live in a shelter, you have to carry your clothes on a backpack, you do not know when you will get out, you do not have a job, child of God, get up, you have the victory. Start praising God; you are coming out. I do not care how long you have been in this situation; the Bible says God knows that you need to eat, dress, and sleep, and He will take care of you. God is always on time. He will not leave you an orphan. He is your everlasting Father. Wouldn't you have trusted your biological father? Trust God more than you would trust in a human being? Okay, you say your biological parents abused you physically, mentally, and sexually, and you don't feel like living anymore. Today, I say start using those gut-punching phrases and stand up. You will be made whole in the name of Jesus. God will take you out of these situations or that mental prison that you have been in for so long.

"Okay," you say, "but you don't know that my family was involved in witchcraft, and I see demons coming to oppress me; I can't sleep at night; I have nightmares of demons persecuting me always." Listen to me: He who is with you is greater than who he is in the world. God is about to strengthen you to have victory, even in your dreams, while you are sleeping. Start now, "I have the victory." Start praising God, for you have come out; you are coming out of your storm. God is your Jehovah Nissi; He will always protect you. He is Jehovah Jireh; He will always provide. He is your protector, your victory, your everlasting Father, your covering. Trust God. Write down or type these in big characters and place them in a place where you can always see them: I am more than a conqueror, I am an overcomer, I am a child of God, I am an heir with Jesus.

> And I am convinced that nothing can ever separate us from God's love. Neither death nor life, neither angels nor demons, neither our fears for today nor our worries about tomorrow—not even the powers of hell can separate us from God's love. No power in the sky above or in the earth below—indeed, nothing in all creation will ever be able to separate us from the love of God that is revealed in Christ Jesus our Lord's Christ, adopted into the family of God, grafted.

> **ROMANS 8:38–39 (NLT)**

Two of my favorite verses in the Bible.

I can assure you that according to the Word of God, "Can anything ever separate us from Christ's love?" (Romans 8:35, NLT). The answer is no. Does it mean that God no longer loves us if we have trouble or calamity, are persecuted, hungry, destitute, in danger, or threatened with death? The Word of God says, "'For your sake we are killed every day; we are being slaughtered like sheep.' No, despite all these things, overwhelming victory is ours through Christ, who loved us" (Romans 8:36–37, NLT). There is a song that I like to listen to and meditate on. It reminds me that I am the reflection of God's glory on this earth. "There Is a River," a song by Bill and Gloria Gaither, reminds us of just that. If you have never heard it, find it now and enjoy the wording of the song; you will be blessed; I guarantee you that.

I pray that these words have been a comfort to you. It is a beautiful song that has gotten me through many depressing moments in my life. When I could not find the strength to pray, this song carried me into the presence of my Savior and allowed me to draw from His strength. Remember, His strength is made perfect in your weakness. But He said to me, "'My grace is sufficient for you, for my power is made perfect in weakness.' Therefore, I will boast all the more gladly about my weaknesses, so that Christ's power may rest on me" (2 Corinthians 12:9, NIV).

Take your Bible and study the verses that apply to your situation by heart. Speak the Word of God. Keep repeating them, reading them, speaking them into the atmosphere. God will do the rest. You need to "Study to shew thyself approved unto God, a workman that needed not to be ashamed, rightly dividing the word of truth" (2 Timothy 2:15, KJV).

CHAPTER 5:

SEEK THE HOLY SPIRIT ON HIM

When Jesus was getting ready to leave the earth and ascend to heaven, He told His disciples that He was leaving, but He would not leave them by themselves, that the Holy Spirit, the Spirit of Truth, the Comforter, would come and will be with them. The Holy Spirit is our firepower. The Bible says, "You shall receive power after that the Holy Ghost has come upon you and you will be my witnesses in Jerusalem, in Samaria and on the extremities of this earth" (Acts 1:8, NIV).

There's one thing I want to explain to you about the Holy Spirit, the person of the Holy Spirit, the Comforter that our Lord Jesus left and sent to be with us. I know that there have been so many misunderstandings about the person of the Holy Spirit and about the pronouns that are used in Christendom when it comes to the Holy Spirit. The Holy Spirit is not an "it" but a person, the third person of the Trinity. Now, let me tell you the Holy Spirit is upon you at salvation because He is the one who brings you to the conviction of God's existence for you to accept Him as your personal Savior. Without the preliminary work of the Holy Spirit, no one would come to know the Lord. The Holy Spirit comes at the time appointed by God; He is upon you for conviction, for belief, and to bring you to the knowledge of Jesus Christ and His work on Calvary. With the help of the Holy Spirit, we are convicted and come closer to God.

The Bible says that the one who comes must believe that He exists and that He is the rewarder of those who diligently seek Him. The Holy Spirit is with you after salvation and is the Helper promised by God. He walks with you, watches over you, leads you, and guides you in all areas of your life. The Holy Spirit becomes your everyday companion and gets you to know Jesus more. He reveals Jesus to you. He brings to your remembrance the things of God. He opens up your spirit to have a great idea of who Jesus Christ is and is with you always until the day of salvation. Who better to teach you about Jesus than the Holy Spirit, our Teacher, our Comforter? The Holy Spirit is upon you for a particular time and for a specific purpose. As an example, when I am in a healing crusade, the Holy Spirit comes upon me at the time when I am ready to pray for the people and brings the saving and miraculous faith to believe in God for any miracle at that particular moment in time. The Bible talks to us about all the specific things that the Holy Spirit does for us in our walk, our life, and our work for God. "But the Helper, the Holy Spirit, whom the Father will send in my name, he will teach you all things and bring to your remembrance all that I have said to you" (John 14:26, ESV).

Have you ever seen a light bulb that does not burn? I remember that when I was a child, they had those light bulbs that, if you touch them, they will burn you. They were so hot. If you put a towel on them, the towel would become so hot, like a warm blanket. As kids, we would place sheets on the light bulb, wait not even a couple of minutes for them to become hot, and we would cover ourselves with the sheets or put them on our skin to warm us up. What does a light bulb have to do with the fire of the Holy Ghost? Nowadays, they make those light bulbs so that although they are very bright, they do not burn. They have fluorescent light bulbs that do not become warm at all. My point is, which light bulb are you? If you are a light that shines, but you do not burn, the enemy is not afraid of you and may harass you at any time. If you are a light bulb that lights up but also becomes hot, the enemy would not dare come near you. I have yet to see a fly go and rest on a hot stove. This is the transformation that the fire and power of the Holy Ghost make in a believer's life. It's the fire that burns if you come too close. As Christians, we should aspire to be baptized in the Holy Ghost and to receive that fire that allows us to operate fully spiritually. That fire puts a stop to the work of the enemy in our lives and the lives of our family members. There is a difference between electrified and electrocuted. We are in the days when the kingdom of hell must be electrocuted, not electrified. We see in the Scriptures,

"For the law of the Spirit of life in Christ Jesus hath made me free from the law of sin and death."

ROMANS 8:2, KJV

"Those who are dominated by sinful nature think about sinful things, but those who are controlled by the Holy Spirit think about things that are pleasing to the Lord. If your sinful nature controls your mind, there is death. But if the Holy Spirit controls your mind, there is life and peace."

ROMANS 8:5–6, NLT

"The Spirit of God, who raised Jesus from the dead, lives in you. And just as he raised Christ from the dead, he will give life to your mortal body by this same Spirit living within you."

ROMANS 8:11, NLT

"For all who are led by the Spirit of God are children of God."

ROMANS 8:14, NLT

"So, you should not be like cowering, fearful slaves. You should behave instead like God's very own children, adopted into his family—calling him 'Father, dear Father.' For his Holy Spirit speaks to us deep in our hearts and tells us that we are God's children" (Romans 8:15–16, NET). These scriptures are powerful and so significant in the work of the Holy Spirit in our lives.

The Holy Spirit is God's gift to all believers. Joel 2:28 (NIV) states, "I will pour out my Spirit upon all people. Your sons and daughters will prophesy. Your old men will dream dreams. Your young men will see visions. In those days, I will pour out my Spirit even on servants, men and women alike." The power of the Holy Spirit is your safeguard, and all His invincibility defends you. If your enemies can overcome omnipotence, then they are able to conquer you. Can they wrestle with Deity and toss Him to the ground? Then they might conquer you. For the power of the Holy Spirit is our power; the power of the Holy Spirit is our might. The Word of God states, "Not by might, not by power but by my Spirit, says the Lord of Hosts" (Zechariah 4:6, ESV).

God has not left you alone.

"But the Counselor, the Holy Spirit, whom the Father will send in my name, will teach you all things and will remind you of everything I have said to you" (John 14:26, CSB). You can do what pleases God because His Spirit gives you power. He is your life and strength. That is why you must not ignore Him or try to live a Christian life without depending on Him. His work will not cease until it is completed at Christ's second coming, when our bodies will be transformed to be like Christ's body (Philippians 3:20–21).

THE HOLY SPIRIT: YOUR FIRE POWER

Let me tell you something. The reason that I can speak to you about storms and some basic biblical principles to apply as you go through a storm is because I have been through storms in my life. In my midnight hour, I looked, and I failed to see who I could turn to minister to me. I cried out to God, "Who would come to minister to me? Who would speak a word of encouragement to me? Who would pray with me?"

I asked God, "I have been there for so many people, helped so many Christians, neglected myself and my family to help others. Who today, Lord, will speak to me and help me?" I had been so deceived by pastors, bishops, prophets, and apostles, disappointed by the actions of the people in the church. I looked, and all I could see was people who wanted more money no matter what, people who were deceiving other people. People who were fakers, people making others believe they have what they don't have, people who have bought demonic powers to entrap the people of God, and I cried, "God." But God has a remnant; do you know what that means? If you are going through a storm and you are feeling disappointed, you don't know who to turn to and where to turn. There are a few people left who are out to experience God, who are hungry and thirsty for God, and there are a few people left who are seeking the heart of God and not His hand. Ask the Holy Spirit to lead you to these people. Ask the Holy Spirit to help you discern the spirits and connect you with the real people of God, the ones who are about God, not money, not materialistic things, not power, nor pride. You will find someone to encourage you, someone to pray with you in agreement. There is a lot of religion out there but not a lot of spirituality, a lot of legalisms but not enough holiness, and many places that are focused on the people creating an outside image that looks good but does not care about the inside. The Bible says man looks on the outside, but God looks at the heart (1 Samuel 16:7).

Establish a relationship with the remnant, which will help you to build yourself up and understand that your storm can never be permanent and God is in control. Your storm will always be a temporary situation. God knows where you are, and He wants to help you. He cares about every detail of your life. He wants the best for you. You may not see it, you may not feel it, but you have to know it. God said it in His Word, and that should settle it in your mind, in your spirit, that it is true. Let the Holy Spirit be a witness to you that the Word of God is true.

Be consumed by it.

Have the Holy Spirit on speed dial!

The Bible says that the Holy Spirit will bring to your remembrance what you already know (John 14:26). Dig deeper into the Word of God to impregnate your own being with the promises and the miracles of God. This exercise will, in turn, strengthen your inner being and strengthen your spirit to be able to deal with your circumstances. In times of war, the soldiers have to be prepared. The United States Army will not send unprepared soldiers to war. There has to be a period of preparation, strength training, then the use of the firearms, and more. The soldiers also report to a captain whom they trust with their lives enough to follow his directives and orders. As you are in a war, you also need to go to boot camp training, with physical endurance and strengthening exercises, learn how to use the fire, and how to rely on the power of God. The Holy Spirit is with you 24/7. Jesus said in the book of John that He is leaving, but He is sending us the Comforter. Rely on the Holy Spirit to be your captain, your general, your colonel, and let

Him direct you and lead you. Follow His instructions carefully, respond to His instructions, and ask Him for help; He is a person.

As stated before, Christians should not continue to make the mistake of referring to the Holy Spirit as an "it" instead of "He." The Holy Spirit is the third person of the Trinity. He is a person, and He resides with you. He is with you to strengthen you if you would let Him. He is with you to guide you and lead you if you accept Him. He is with you to comfort you if you will allow Him. He is with you always until you pass on to glory, which will be when you fall asleep. You are aware that Christians do not die but fall asleep, but that is a subject for my other book. The Holy Spirit is an important part of your walk with God—your steps as a Christian. Being baptized in the Holy Ghost should be a requisite for every Christian. That is where the power lies. When you are baptized in the Holy Ghost with the evidence of speaking in heavenly tongues, your walk is much easier. Do you remember the analogy I made before about the two light bulbs, one that burns and one that does not? Receiving the baptism of the Holy Spirit makes you enter the category of the light bulb that burns when you first touch it, and if you keep this light on by fellowshipping with the remnant, be about the things of God, and obey the principles of God, then the enemy would know that it cannot attack you anyhow. You would avoid many storms and attacks. You would be, and I use these words with caution, a dangerous Christian to the kingdom of darkness. The enemy, as I said before, knows the people he can attack and the ones he runs away from.

One day, a lady called me and asked me to come to her house to pray with her. She felt that she was being oppressed by demonic spirits. I went to her house, and there were many people there catering to her. She was sitting on the floor in a room with no shoes on, and she was crying. Some people were touching her hair, some were holding onto her hand, and some were rubbing her back. As soon as I entered the house, she popped herself up, jumped on her feet, and before I could even get in the room, she cried out, "Pastor Laudz, I hate you, I hate you," with a deep, hoarse voice. And I said, smiling, "You do not even know me, and you hate me."

The demon responded through her, "Oh no, I know you, and I hate you." The enemy knows about you, knows when you are weak to attack to confuse you and to bamboozle you. Contrary to this, the Holy

Spirit knows you, is with you, and will be upon you when you need His power to sustain you. Develop your relationship with the Holy Spirit; He is your Helper whom the Master has given to you to lighten your burden and your walk with God. Use Him, let Him direct you, and be attentive to His commands. They are from God. The Holy Spirit is connected to heaven and knows the will of the Father for your life, and He is connected to you to ensure that God's will manifests in your life. He is your fire. He is your power. Combined, He is your firepower that will be able to sustain you from the fiery arrows of the enemy. Trust the Holy Spirit in your everyday life activities. He wants to direct you in everything, from where your feet will touch to whom you will marry to what to study, and He will help you to be strengthened inside out. He is your inner strength.

CHAPTER 6 :

HELP OTHERS THROUGH THEIR STORMS

One of the major things that will constantly help in your storms is when you decide to come out of yourself and help others. Helping others is such a fulfilling and rewarding experience; it will not allow you to dwell on your circumstances but help you to endure and persevere with strength. Do you know that whatever you are going through, someone is going through something harder? You might say, "How does that help me in my storm, in my situation?" There is something marvelous about being able to bring help to somebody else, something that would strengthen you, so when you are able to, look past your dramatic situation and into someone else. There is comfort in doing so and gratitude from the person that you would have helped. The Bible says in 2 Corinthians 1:4 (NLT), "He comforts us in all our troubles so that we can comfort others. When they are troubled, we will be able to give them the same comfort God has given us."

I have to tell you, if you are going through a storm right now, you might not want to believe that, but we benefit a lot from being carried through storms, trials, and tribulations. We learn to depend on God more fully, and we trust Him more fully. Sometimes, we go through storms not for ourselves but for the benefit of others. It is because the Lord wants to position us to help others. Whatever the reason that you are going through a storm, it will work out for your good, and the name of the Lord will be glorified if you keep on trusting Him. When we come to the realization that these things work in us a far greater and eternal weight of glory, we can rejoice in these times. When we look through our eyes of faith, we can see past the storms and see Jesus standing at the end of the storms, waiting for us. Remember that God is in control, and there is nothing that we can go through where He would not carry us. Nothing is too hard for God. God comforts us when we are in a storm so that we can, in turn, comfort others. We suffer sometimes for others' benefit.

A great example is in the word is Joseph. Joseph was sold into slavery by his own brothers and taken to Egypt. He was sold and promoted in the house of Potiphar but then falsely accused and imprisoned for years. God promoted Joseph from prison to palace, from dungeons to diadems. He became the second most powerful man in Egypt. And when the drought came, Joseph was able to send for his family and provide for them. He received them into the land of Egypt, including his brothers, who betrayed him. God worked it out for their good and for the needs of His people. But notice that it was also for the needs of others. God allowed Joseph to understand and interpret Pharaoh's dream, and because of that, the food that was placed in storage in the years of plenty sustained many when the famine came, including the people of Egypt. I am sharing this with you so that you can rejoice even in the storms, knowing that God is working it out for your good and also for the good of others.

> Not only that, but we rejoice in our sufferings, knowing that suffering produces endurance, and endurance produces character, and character

produces hope, and hope does not put us to shame, because God's love has been poured into our hearts through the Holy Spirit who has been given to us.

You go through storms so that you can be perfected, established, strengthened, and settled in Christ.

When God called me into the ministry, He gave me that verse, which at the time really scared me. "I have refined you, but not as silver is refined. Rather, I have refined you in the furnace of suffering" (Isaiah 48:10, NLT). I started crying out to God, saying to Him, "There are verses in the Bible where You refined people like gold, but You want to refine me through afflictions." In prayer, God shared with me that He would refine me through afflictions because He wanted to make sure that when His children came to me for help, I would not take them lightly. I would understand their pain, have compassion, and help them. When the storms came, I did not know if I would make it. I kept crying to God, "Will I make it?" My strength was gone, and I was left like a spiritual destitute. I realized at some point that I was taking my storms personally but that I was going through the refinement process that God had told me at the beginning, and victory was forthcoming. I started to look at the storms with eyes of understanding, and I started looking forward to the end of the storm because I knew what was waiting for me was beyond anything that I could ever imagine. I began to let this verse penetrate my inner being and take root in my spirit: "But, as it is written, 'What no eye has seen, nor ear heard, nor the heart of man imagined, what God has prepared for those who love him'" (1 Corinthians 2:9, ESV). I was anticipating and glad to have gone through the storms, and I was coming out.

David says in the book of Psalms, "It was good for me to be afflicted so that I might learn your decrees. The law from your mouth is more precious to me than thousands of pieces of silver and gold" (Psalm 119:71–72, NIV). Psalm 23, which is a very familiar psalm, states in verse 4, "Even though I walk through the valley of the shadow of death, I will fear no evil, for you are with me; your rod and your staff, they comfort me" (Psalm 23:4, ESV). I heard a man give a testimony one time that he grew up in church, but as he got older, he fell for the trap of the world and its pleasures. His mother was a prayer warrior who was always on her knees, asking God to please save her son. He related that his mother taught him the importance of studying the Psalms from an early age, but the only Psalm he could ever remember was Psalm 23. One night, he reported he had been out until the wee hours of the night when he met with some demonic figures who told him that it was the end for him. They managed to explain to him that they were about to kill him and that his family would never see him again. Scared beyond what one can imagine, he started praying Psalm 23, and he said when he got to the point of saying, "Even though I walked through the valley of death, I shall fear no evil," he felt himself being lifted, and when he opened his eyes, he was standing in front of his mother's house. God had provided for him and saved him from his enemies. God will also do it for you. He is no respecter of persons. What He does for one, He will do it for the other. Do not fear as you go through your storm; God will also stand and provide for you in every way, financially, physically, emotionally, and mentally. God is the one who can turn your mess into a message, your test into a testimony, and take you from a victim to a victor. First Peter 1:6–7 says,

> In this you greatly rejoice, even though now for a little while, if necessary, you have been distressed by various trials, so that the proof of your faith, being more precious than gold which is perishable, even though tested by fire, may be

found to result in praise and glory and honor at the revelation of Jesus Christ.

1 PETER 1:6–7 (NASB)

The true believer's faith will be strengthened by the storms they experience so that they can rest in the knowledge that it is genuine and will last forever. However, I want to emphasize that we should never make excuses for our storms. If they are a result of our own wrongdoings, we will pay the natural consequences of our actions even though God has forgiven us because of Jesus's sacrifice on the cross. We have been spared eternal punishment due to the blood of Jesus that was shed for us. First Peter 4:15 (NIV) says, "If you suffer, it should not be as a murderer or thief or any other kind of criminal, or even as a meddler."

Storms come into your life with both a purpose and a reward. Throughout any storm, we know, undoubtedly, that we have the victory. God will not allow us to be tested beyond what He knows we can bear, as evidenced in the book of 1 Corinthians 10:13 (ESV): "No temptation has overtaken you that is not common to man. God is faithful, and he will not let you be tempted beyond your ability, but with the temptation he will also provide the way of escape, that you may be able to endure it." Become an encourager.

How do you do this? How do you encourage one in need of encouragement? We can look at someone in the Bible. He was born Joses but is more known by the name of Barnabas. The Bible's records of this man's life show him as a man who liked to encourage others. In the book of Acts, Chapter 9:26–27, after Saul was converted, he tried to unite himself with the other disciples who were in Jerusalem, but out of fear and prejudice about his past, they were afraid to allow him into their group. However, Barnabas came to Saul's side, stood up for him, and told the others about the man's amazing conversion. He stood up for one who desperately needed a friend. Through your storm, learn to encourage others. Try to take the time to reach out to those around you who seem to be lonely or who have been rejected by others. Look around you. There are plenty of people who would benefit and be grateful for your help. Be a friend to someone who needs a friend.

In the book of Acts 11, when the church in Jerusalem heard that there was a new group of believers in Antioch, they sent Barnabas to them to help them along. The Bible tells us that when he arrived, he exhorted them. That means he encouraged them. He was excited about what God was doing and how these new converts were serving the Lord, and he did his best to encourage them to carry on. Help someone in their walk with God. Encourage someone in their faith. It will do wonders for you in your storm.

In the book of Acts 15:35–40, Paul, Barnabas, and John Mark were together on a missionary journey. For some reason, John Mark left them and returned to Jerusalem (Acts 13:13). Now, Paul and Barnabas were ready to go out again, and Barnabas wanted to take John Mark along to give him a second chance. Paul disagreed, and he and Barnabas parted company (Acts 15:36–40). Paul took Silas and went out with him, while Barnabas took John Mark and disappeared from the biblical account.

While Barnabas is never heard from again, his ministry to John Mark had far-reaching consequences! Because Barnabas gave this discouraged and defeated young man a second chance, his life as a servant of God was salvaged. In fact, before Paul died in Rome, he requested that Mark be sent to him (2 Timothy 4:11). Even more important is the fact that because Barnabas took the time to encourage a discouraged brother, Mark was used by the Lord to pen the Gospel of Mark, which gives us an exciting account of the life and ministry of the Lord Jesus Christ.

While you are going through this storm, find someone who is going through the same things you are going through, unite, start a group, and pray together. Reach out to the discouraged, the ones people have washed their hands off of, and be an encourager to them.

Give yourself freely to the work of God, promote it, encourage it, and praise and worship God. It will help take your mind off your storms, and you will be strengthened and encouraged. Encourage yourself in the Lord. There is an amazing story of someone who went through a storm, and his reaction is priceless in the book of 1 Samuel, Chapter 30, verses 1–6:

> And it came to pass, when David and his men were come to Ziklag on the third day, that the Amalekites had invaded the south, and Ziklag, and smitten Ziklag, and burned it with fire.
>
> And had taken the women captives, that were therein: they slew not any, either great or small, but carried them away, and went on their way. So David and his men came to the city, and, behold, it was burned with fire; and their wives, and their sons, and their daughters, were taken captives. Then David and the people that were with him lifted up their voice and wept, until they had no more

power to weep. And David's two wives were taken captives, Ahinoam the Jezreelitess, and Abigail the wife of Nabal the Carmelite. And David was greatly distressed; for the people spake of stoning him, because the soul of all the people was grieved, every man for his sons and for his daughters: but David encouraged himself in the LORD his God.

1 SAMUEL 30:1–6 (KJV)

There was a war between Amalek and Israel since Israel was to destroy the Amalekites. And it is written He said, "Because hands were lifted up against the throne of the LORD, the LORD will be at war against the Amalekites from generation to generation" (Exodus 17:16, NIV).

The men came back; they were tired and weary after a long march with Achish and then another long journey home. They longed to sit and rest! They wanted to see their wives and their children, I am sure, and be comforted! Tears did not seem a sufficient expression for their pain, and yet we see these men of war cry and weep, warriors like Joab, coarse men like Abishai, or men like Asahel. This was beside what they had expected, and they were grieving. They cried until they had no more strength to weep.

David was in a bind. He had to deal with his own personal sorrow, but that of all his people; and moreover, instead of standing with him, every friend had turned into an enemy; his house was a heap of ashes; he might have said, "Ahinoam is not, and Abigail is not, and my children have been taken away; all these things are against me!" But he had more faith than Job, and so he encouraged himself in the Lord his God. What a mess of a storm, but in all things, we trust God. God came through for David and gave him the victory more than he asked for. He will do the same for you.

CHAPTER 7:

GET BETTER, NOT BITTER

The best revenge against the attacks of the enemy is to get better, not bitter. Let your anger arise and decide that you will not fall into the plan of the enemy but that you will use your storm period to become more intimate with your Father in heaven. Become a better Christian, a better friend, a better mother, a better father, a better teacher. Resolve that you will allow the Lord to take you to another level in Him. Face your fears and stand firm. Tell the devil what he meant for evil, God will turn around for your good. "Let me illustrate this further. Who is powerful enough to enter the house of a strong man like Satan and plunder his goods? Only someone even stronger—someone who could tie him up and then plunder his house" (Mark 3:27, NLT).

Think about your storm. How do you learn from

it? How do we become better in order not to become bitter? God does not look upon our problems as we do. Where we see stress, He sees opportunities. When we see crisis, He sees growth. God's purpose in times of storms is to teach His children wonderful and precious lessons. The storms are intended to instruct us and shape us up. And when we open our hearts to learn from them and ride out the storms of life, we see the promises fulfilled in our lives...We need to discover the joy in times of trouble, seize the moment, and learn. In the end, we will realize that our storms had been necessary to arm us, to give us the necessary ammunition to fight our enemy. Our faith will be fortified; we will learn to rely on God more than our own physical abilities, and more than that, we will know not to fall for the devices of the enemy because our victory was won at Calvary.

Refuse to be bitter. You have a choice: become better or bitter (Job 21:25; Hebrews 12:15). How can you avoid bitterness? Accept what cannot be changed (Job 11:13, 16). Focus on what you still have, not what you have lost (1 Thessalonians 5:18).

CHAPTER 8:

IT'S
THANKING
TIME

I do not like to go through trials, and for many years, I would try and try to get out of a storm more than anything. I would be so happy when the storm was over. Moreover, I would be crying out to God, travailing before God to get me out of the storm. I did not care about anything other than coming out of the storm. Storms kept happening in my life, and sometimes, the same storms would duplicate themselves. The storms became harder to handle, more difficult in nature. The fights became stronger and stronger. Finally, I was forced to rethink my strategy and my attitude toward the storm and come in alignment with Scripture that the purpose of a storm is to be educated, learn valuable lessons, and grow in maturity and faith. I began to expect something different from my storms, knowing that God was in control.

I learned to rely on Him more and more in the knowledge that He will never leave me nor forsake me. I took courage in knowing that I needed to go through these storms, that the end result would always be a blessing for me, and that the name of God would be glorified. I came to understand that as the scripture says, "I give them eternal life, and they shall never perish; no one will snatch them out of my hand" (John 10:28, NIV). "I will never leave you nor forsake you" takes a new meaning in my being, and today, I am prepared when the storms come because I know a greater blessing is awaiting me on the other end of the storm. Today, I can praise Him and worship Him. Oh, that you would come to the knowledge of God and understand Him, be intimate with Him to the point that a storm does not scare you, a storm does not stress you but to welcome the opportunity to be challenged to go higher, to receive more grace and to reach another level spiritually. Oh, that you would get to know that God is love. His thoughts toward you are not to harm you in any way but to embrace you and love you. That you would come to know Him, your Father, who loves you so much He sacrificed His unique Son to save you so that He could have fellowship with you. Oh, that you would come to know Him as the All-Powerful, Almighty God who cares so much for His children and wants the best out of them. I can tell you that God wants you to succeed. Instead of fighting your storm, allow it to run its course. Start thanking God today that He has kept you through the storms, start thanking God for the valuable lessons you have learned, and start thanking God for you being a more mature Christian today than you were when your storm started. Praise the name of the Lord, for He is good, and His mercies endure forever.

Psalm 139 states that you are wonderfully made; you are made in the image of God. Have you ever looked at yourself in a mirror? What you are looking at is a reflection of God. It is time to thank God that He sustained you during the storm. Your mess has turned into a message.

You need to see life as a series of problem-solving and opportunities to learn and grow. The storms that we face will either empower us or overcome and overwhelm us. Do not choose to keep thinking about your problem, therefore making it impossible for you to see the hand of God in your life. I want so deeply to convey the love of Jesus Christ to you. I want so much to let you know that He loves you. You are engraved in the palm of His hand. He can never forget you. Give Him praise and worship. The Bible says to enter His gates with thanksgiving and His courts with praise.

Remember what is important in life. And guess what, it is not our things and stuff. It is not career, cars, boats, toys, education, looks, power, or status. It is relationships, not things, that matter (Luke 12:15; 1 Timothy 6:7).

Focus on Christ. This is the secret reservoir of strength we have access to. This gives us perseverance in tough times (Philippians 4:13).

GOD USES PROBLEMS TO SHIELD YOU FROM GREATER HARM

Problems can be a blessing in disguise because they can prevent us from being harmed by something more severe, such as a car breaking down just before it reaches the railroad tracks as a train is zooming by. Car breakdowns are stressful and costly, but the train is even more so. Just as in the story of Joseph, where he suffered needlessly from our perspective but God protected him and turned it into incredibly good.

GOD USES PROBLEMS TO REFINE AND IMPROVE YOU

Problems are the main ingredients for us to build character. The key to these building materials is that they need to be used in the right way to be able to fit and function correctly. And that right way is how we respond and learn. God is far more interested in our character than our comfort. In the grand scheme of things, the meaning of life, the reason we live the life we are given, is our relationship with God and then others around us. So, the most important thing we have in those relationships is our character; the only two things we will take into eternity are relationships and character.

"We can rejoice when we run into problems... they help us learn to be patient and patience develops strength of character in us and helps us trust God more each time we use it until finally our hope and faith are strong and steady" (Romans 5:3–4, TLB).

Remember this main point: God is at work in your life, even when you cannot see Him. We will go through trials and suffering because of the sin that has infected the world and us. We will grow best for His glory by recognizing and confessing sin. Then, we can grow even more when we learn and mature from those experiences. You will have far more contentment and joy in your life when you cooperate and allow God's love to rule in your life and surrender your fears, desires, and pain to Him.

CHAPTER 9:

NO STORY,
NO GLORY

Our primary goal is to learn from our mistakes and experiences so we can grow in our faith and practice for His glory.

Ask God to ease your grief. This is not denying it or ignoring your crisis; you are going through it for a reason. But as David did, tell God exactly how you feel. Use this to enhance your relationship with Him (Psalm 34:18; Psalm 62:8).

I say it again, and I continue to say it, remember what is important in life. And guess what, it is not our things and stuff. It is not career, cars, boats, toys, education, looks, power, or status. It is relationships, not things, that matter (Luke 12:15; 1 Timothy 6:7).

Focus on Christ. This is the secret reservoir of strength we have access to. This gives us perseverance in tough times (Philippians 4:13).

HOW DO I DO THIS?

- *Place your trust and reliance upon Christ*; this is where your stability comes from (Isaiah 26:3; Psalm 112:6–7, 125:1).

- *Learn to listen* to our Lord through your prayers and devotions. And to godly advice. This is where our direction comes from (Jeremiah 29:11).

- *Look to Christ for salvation!* God is our Redemption, so because of what He did, we can draw our strength from Him and rest in His protection. Remember, He always helps in times of trouble; if you do not see it, then you are not looking (Psalm 46:2).

There is no glory without a story.

So when God tests you or bad stuff happens, you need to see it as a time for you to learn and to trust Him by changing what is wrong with you while putting His promises in your heart and feet. And when it is over, you can look back and see that your trials have been necessary. You are better; He is glorified!

We must first adjust the way we perceive life. Even as Christians, sometimes we have faulty views and expectations we pick up by listening to bad teaching and bad advice, and then there is the influence of our culture. First of all, bad things do happen! And they happen to good people (in the way we see good; in God's eyes, of course, all have sinned, and there is no good, except what Christ brings us). We will go through trials, troubles, and tribulations. So, what we have to do is figure out what we do when it happens.

Some people go through oppositions, but they do not have a story; some people go through storms, but they do not have a story; some people are wounded badly, but they do not have a story. If you do not have a story, it would be very difficult for you to see the glory of God. God will put us through things so that we can give Him all the glory. The Bible says in Psalm 103:7 (ESV), "He made known his ways to Moses his acts to the people of Israel." Moses did not see God, but he saw God's glory. The children of Israel only knew His works, meaning His miracles, but they did not know Him. Do you want to see the glory of God? Do you want to know Him? If there is no story, there is no glory. But if you know your God, He is the Lily of the Valley, the Bright Morning Star, the Rose of Sharon. He will never leave you nor forsake you. Moses was a simple man who loved God, who spoke to God and is recorded as God speaking to him as with a friend. In Exodus 33:18–19 (NET),

"Moses said, 'Please show me your glory.' And he said, 'I will make all my goodness pass before you and will proclaim before you my name 'The Lord.' And I will be gracious to whom I will be gracious and will show mercy on whom I will show mercy."

What about the story of Lazarus? Lazarus and his two (2) sisters were friends of Jesus. When Lazarus fell ill, they sent a message to Jesus, "Lord, the one you love is sick." On the first day, He did not go; on the second day, He did not go; on the third day, Jesus made His way to Lazarus's hometown of Bethany. Jesus knew that the name of God would be glorified by this great miracle that He was about to perform. When Jesus arrived at Bethany, Lazarus had already died and had been in the tomb for four (4) days. When Martha heard that Jesus was on the way, she went out to meet Him. "Lord, she said if you had been there, my brother would not have died." Jesus told Martha, "Your brother will rise again." But Martha thought He was talking about the resurrection from the dead. Then Jesus said these important words, "I am the resurrection and the life. He who believes in Me will live even though he dies, and whoever lives and believes in Me will never die."

Martha then went and told Mary that Jesus

wanted to see her. Jesus had not yet entered the village, most likely to avoid stirring up the crowd and bring attention to Himself. The town of Bethany was not far from Jerusalem, where the Jewish leaders were plotting against Jesus. When Mary met Jesus, she was grieving with strong emotion over her brother's death. The Jews with her were also weeping and mourning. Deeply moved by their grief, Jesus wept with them. Jesus then went to the tomb of Lazarus with Mary, Martha, and the rest of the mourners. He asked them to remove the stones that covered the hillside burial place. Jesus looked up to heaven and prayed to His Father, ending with these words, "Lazarus, come forward." When Lazarus came out of the tomb, Jesus instructed the people to take off his grave clothes. Many people put their faith in Jesus after that. There needs to be a story for glory.

The following story is reported from a great healing evangelist, Smith Wigglesworth.

One day, he and his wife received a letter from a young man asking for prayer. He had been healed about three years before of a bad foot, and they had lost all trace of him since, until this urgent cry came from a home where, in the natural, death was soon to enter. When the letter came, Mrs. Wigglesworth said to her husband, "If you go, God will give you this case." He telegraphed he would go and started riding from Grantham, nine miles away, to Willsford on his bicycle. When he reached the village, he inquired where the young man, Matthew Snell, lived. He had heart failure and had to lie perfectly still in one place. The doctor said if he moved from that place, he would die, and he left him, never expecting to see him alive again. When Mr. Wigglesworth reached the house, the mother of the young man stood in the doorway and said, "Oh, you have come too late."

"Is he alive at all?" was asked.

"Yes, he is just alive."

He went into the parlor where he was lying. The young man, Matthew, said in a low voice, "I cannot rise. I am too weak, and the doctor says if I turn around, I shall die." Mr. Wigglesworth said this to him, "Matthew, the Lord is the strength of thy heart and thy portion altogether. Will you believe that the Lord will raise you up for His glory?" The young man answered, "Lord, if You will raise me up for Your glory, I will give You my life." Hands were laid on him in the name of the Lord Jesus, and instantly, new life came into him.

"Shall I arise?" he asked, but the ministering servant felt he should lie perfectly quiet as so advised. The night was spent in prayer, and the next morning, Brother Wigglesworth attended the ten o'clock meeting in the Primitive Methodist Chapel. He was asked to speak and talked of faith in God, and from that moment, the unbelief seemed to clear away from the village people. They came to him at the close of the service and said, "We believe Matthew will be raised up." He had asked the family to air Matthew's clothing for him to put on, but they didn't do it because they did not believe he would be restored. For six weeks, he had been in a serious condition, becoming weaker all the time. Mr. Wigglesworth insisted on their airing Matthew's clothing, and they did it, not because they believed in healing but to satisfy him.

At about 2:30, he went into the room where the young man lay and said, "Now, I would like this to be for the glory of God. It shall never be said that Wigglesworth raised you up." The young man answered, "For Thy glory, Lord; my life shall be for Thee." Then the servant of the Lord said, "Matthew, I believe the moment I lay hands on you, the glory of God will fill this place, so I shall not be able to stand."

As he did this, the glory of the Lord fell upon them until he fell on his face to the floor; it increased until everything in the room shook, the bed and Matthew who was on the bed, and with a strong voice, the young man cried out, "For Thy glory, Lord! For Thy glory!" This continued for at least fifteen minutes, when it was apparent to them God would give him strength not only to rise but to dress in the glorious power, which seemed like the description given of the temple being filled with the glory of God and the young man was walking up and down, shouting and praising God and clapping his hands. He went to the door and called to his father that the Lord had raised him up. His father was a backslider and fell down before God and cried for mercy. His sister, who had been brought out of an asylum and was threatened with another attack of insanity, in the manifestation of that glory was delivered from that time. That weak body immediately became strong, eating regular food immediately. The doctor came and examined his heart and declared it was all right. Matthew declared it should be for the Lord's glory and at once began preaching in the power of the Holy Ghost. His own statement is that when he gives the story of his healing, many are saved.

Yes, you have been through storms, but there is a purpose to your storm. You have a story; you will experience God's glory. So many times, men and women go through bad experiences, and it ends up being the area of ministry that God wants to use for His glory. Who can better understand an addict than someone who has been addicted? Who can better understand a prostitute than someone who prostituted themselves? Who can better have compassion for a homeless person besides the Lord than someone who understands what it is to be homeless? And the list continues. Lonely? Rejected? Humiliated? Bamboozled? Mental health issues? Divorce? We go through storms for ourselves, for others, for the ministry, and always for the glory of God. The Bible states, "Where sin abounded, grace did much more abound" (Romans 5:20, KJV).

I cannot miss out on telling you about the grace of God that will carry you in any situation. The grace of God is unmerited favor. God does not do you good because He is under constraint to do. He does because He wants to and because He is God all by Himself. He has chosen to use men and have fellowship with them. The book of Zephaniah states, "The LORD your God is in your midst, a mighty one who will save; he will rejoice over you with gladness; he will quiet you by his love; he will exult over you with loud singing" (Zephaniah 3:17, ESV). I pray that as you read this and as you have gained an understanding of your storms, trials, tribulations, and how and why we go through them, you will proclaim with the apostle Paul: "But by the grace of God I am what I am, and his grace toward me was not in vain. On the contrary, I worked harder than any of them, though it was not I, but the grace of God that is with me" (1 Corinthians 15:10, ESV).

CHAPTER 10:

ELIMINATE
YOUR
DISTRACTIONS

When I started writing this book, I wanted to empower the people of God to become all that God intended for them to be. I have been to so many churches to preach and teach from different walks of life, different cultures, and different nationalities, and one thing that always saddens me is the look on the faces of some of the people of God. They look and feel defeated; they are stressed and distressed. The enemy has their back on the wall, and it looks like they have lost faith and trust in God. My goal was to create a book that would be powerful enough and easy to understand enough that people would know that they can never be defeated with God. Christians are sleeping because the enemy of our souls has found ways to convince them that he is in control of their lives. Life has become so difficult, and as sickness, disease, infirmity, high prices, tornados, hurricanes, and earthquakes are keeping our minds busy, we tend to focus less and less on Jesus. Jesus is the answer. No man has the answer, but God. God is the one that is able. He is a covenant-keeping God. He will never betray His Word. "God *is* not a man, that He should lie, nor a son of man, that He should repent. Has He said, and will He not do? Or has He spoken, and will He not make it good? God has you" (Numbers 23:19, NKJV).

Distraction is a major weapon of the enemy. Do not allow yourself to be distracted from the plan of God for your life. Now that you have applied these nuggets of wisdom and you have come out of your storm, stay focused on Jesus Christ. Let Him fill your life with His love. One day, as I was going through a storm, I was desperate. I kept crying out to God, "Will I make it? Will I come out of it?" I did not see the way out, and I was spending my days in despair. As I was sitting, crawling on the floor in my room, just being distressed, trying to read the Bible, but the words were not even penetrating my spirit, I was in a state of despair. I felt that warmth covering my entire body. I thought I had reached heaven. This warm presence covered me like a blanket of love, so caring beyond anything that I could ever describe here. It was like Jesus was telling me, "I love you so much," and He enveloped me with His caring love, His caring nature. It felt like only a second, and the presence lifted, leaving me just wanting to experience it repeatedly.

I said to myself, "Is it what it feels like to be in heaven?" From that time, I decided that I would not miss heaven, that I would serve God with all my being, and that whatever God wanted me to do, I would do. I am God's servant. I am His slave and His mouthpiece. Whatever He wants me to do, that is what I will do. My desire is for you to experience the love of God. It is such a burden in my heart for the world to know that God is powerful. The one that they are rejecting, He is the one that allows them to even be on this earth. There is a difference between an evangelist and a prophet. An evangelist has a burden for the lost souls and wants to see them saved; a prophet has a burden for the people of God and wants to encourage them, exhort them, and put them on the path to their divine destiny.

If I have done anything, I pray that through my words, my experiences, biblical principles, and truths, I have been able to instill in you the strength to go through any storms that will come your way, knowing that God has the wheel in His hands. "As for the appearance of the wheels and their construction: their appearance was like the gleaming of beryl. And the four had the same likeness, their appearance and construction being as it were a wheel within a wheel" (Ezekiel 1:16, ESV).

It is my hope that all aspects of this book will become a place of encouragement to all who read it and a way to have their mind renewed and transformed by the Word of God.

You have won the battle, and the storm subsided. The devil will have new tricks and distractions to try to get you back into a place of despair. But you are better equipped! You know the tricks and apply the nuggets of wisdom, stay connected to the Vine always, and you will not forget all that you learned through your storm and backslide. You are stronger in Him!

IN SUMMARY

1. Take care of God's business. He will take care of yours (help others);

2. Get involved;

3. Address any issues; do not dwell in pity parties.

4. Get the right perspective of the storm. The wrong perspective will create further issues (Job and his friends).

AFTER THE STORM

1. Thanksgiving;

2. If it was a test, you have a testimony;

3. If it was a mess, message of victory.

LESSONS FROM A STORM

1. Moving on (reaching your God-given destiny);

2. Continually use the Word of God;

3. Use words of encouragement.

EPILOGUE

ENCOURAGING VERSES

I have included some verses that have sustained and strengthened me and will do the same for you in your times of tests and trials.

"The LORD replied, 'My Presence will go with you, and I will give you rest.'"

EXODUS 33:14, CSB

"Be strong and courageous. Do not be afraid or terrified because of them, for the LORD your God goes with you; he will never leave you nor forsake you."

DEUTERONOMY 31:6, NIV

"The Lord himself goes before you and will be with you; he will never leave you nor forsake you. Do not be afraid; do not be discouraged."

DEUTERONOMY 31:8, NIV

"Have I not commanded you? Be strong and courageous. Do not be afraid; do not be discouraged, for the LORD your God will be with you wherever you go."

JOSHUA 1:9, NIV

"This day is holy to our Lord. Do not grieve, for the joy of the LORD is your strength."

NEHEMIAH 8:10B, NKJV

"When his lamp shone on my head and by his light I walked through darkness!"

JOB 29:3, NIV

The LORD is my shepherd, I lack nothing.
    He makes me lie down in green pastures,

he leads me beside quiet waters,
    he refreshes my soul.

He guides me along the right paths
    for his name's sake.

Even though I walk
    through the darkest valley,

I will fear no evil,
    for you are with me;

your rod and your staff,
    they comfort me.

You prepare a table before me
    in the presence of my enemies.

You anoint my head with oil;
    my cup overflows.

Surely your goodness and love will follow me
    all the days of my life,

and I will dwell in the house of the LORD forever.

PSALM 23 (NIV)

The Lord is my light and my salvation—
whom shall I fear?

The Lord is the stronghold of my life—
of whom shall I be afraid?

PSALM 27:1 (NIV)

Though an army besiege me,
my heart will not fear;
though war break out against me,
even then I will be confident.

PSALM 27:3 (NIV)

You are my hiding place;
you will protect me from trouble
and surround me with songs of deliverance.

I will instruct you and teach you in the way you
should go;

I will counsel you with my loving eye on you.

PSALM 32:7–8 (NIV)

"Trust in the LORD and do good; dwell in the land and enjoy safe pasture. Take delight in the LORD, AND he will give you the desires of your heart. Commit your way to the LORD; TRUST in him and he will do this."

PSALM 37:3–5, NIV

Be still before the LORD and wait patiently for
him; do not fret when people succeed in their ways,
when they carry out their wicked schemes. Refrain
from anger and turn from wrath; do not fret—it
leads only to evil. For those who are evil will be
destroyed, but those who hope in the LORD will
inherit the land.

PSALM 37:7–9 (NIV)

As the deer pants for streams of water,
    so my soul pants for you, my God.

My soul thirsts for God, for the living God.
    When can I go and meet with God?

My tears have been my food
    day and night,

while people say to me all day long,
    "Where is your God?"

These things I remember
    as I pour out my soul:

how I used to go to the house of God
    under the protection of the Mighty One

with shouts of joy and praise
    among the festive throng.

Why, my soul, are you downcast?
    Why so disturbed within me?

Put your hope in God,
    for I will yet praise him,
        my Savior and my God.

My soul is downcast within me;
   therefore I will remember you
from the land of the Jordan,
   the heights of Hermon—from Mount Mizar.
Deep calls to deep
   in the roar of your waterfalls;
all your waves and breakers
   have swept over me.

By day the Lord directs his love,
   at night his song is with me—
   a prayer to the God of my life.

I say to God my Rock,
   "Why have you forgotten me?
Why must I go about mourning,
   oppressed by the enemy?"
My bones suffer mortal agony
   as my foes taunt me,
saying to me all day long,
   "Where is your God?"

Why, my soul, are you downcast?
   Why so disturbed within me?
Put your hope in God,
   for I will yet praise him,
   my Savior and my God.

PSALM 42 (NIV)

Hear my cry, O God; listen to my prayer. From the ends of the earth I call to you, I call as my heart grows faint; lead me to the rock that is higher than I. For you have been my refuge, a strong tower against the foe. Long to dwell in your tent forever and take refuge in the shelter of your wings.

PSALM 61:1–4 (ESV)

Praise the Lord, my soul, and forget not all his benefits—who forgives all your sins and heals all your diseases, who redeems your life from the pit and crowns you with love and compassion, who satisfies your desires with good things so that your youth is renewed like the eagle's.

PSALM 103:2–5 (NIV)

"Though I walk in the midst of trouble, you preserve my life. You stretch out your hand against the anger of my foes; with your right hand you save me."

PSALM 138:7, NIV

"The Lord is near to all who call on him, to all who call on him in truth. He fulfills the desires of those who fear him; he hears their cry and saves them."

PSALM 145:18–19, NIV

"He heals the brokenhearted and binds up their wounds."

PSALM 147:3, NIV

"Trust in the Lord with all your heart and lean not on your own understanding; in all your ways submit to him, and he will make your paths straight."

PROVERBS 3:5–6, NIV

"The name of the Lord is a fortified tower; the righteous run to it and are safe"

PROVERBS 18:10, NIV

"Fear of man will prove to be a snare, but whoever trusts in the Lord is kept safe."

PROVERBS 29:25, NIV

"Do not be like them, for your father knows what you need before you ask him."

MATTHEW 6:8, NIV

So do not worry, saying, "What shall we eat?" or "What shall we drink?" or "What shall we wear?" For the pagans run after all these things, and your heavenly Father knows that you need them. But seek first his kingdom and his righteousness, and all these things will be given to you as well. Therefore do not worry about tomorrow, for tomorrow will worry about itself. Each day has enough trouble of its own.

MATTHEW 6:31–34 (NIV)

"Are not five sparrows sold for two pennies? Yet not one of them is forgotten by God. Indeed, the very hairs of your head are all numbered. Don't be afraid; you are worth more than many sparrows."

LUKE 12:6–7, NIV

"Who of you by worrying can add a single hour to your life? Since you cannot do this very little thing, why do you worry about the rest?"

LUKE 12:25–26, NIV

"Do not be afraid, little flock, for your Father has been pleased to give you the kingdom."

LUKE 12:32, NIV

"Peace, I leave with you; my peace I give you. I do not give to you as the world gives. Do not let your heart be troubled and do not be afraid."

JOHN 14:27, NIV

"I consider that our present sufferings are not worth comparing with the glory that will be revealed in us."

ROMANS 8:18, NIV

"And we know that in all things God works for the good of those who love him, who have been called according to his purpose."

ROMANS 8:28, NIV

"What, then, shall we say in response to these things? If God is for us, who can be against us?"

ROMANS 8:31, NIV

"Who shall separate us from the love of Christ? Shall trouble or hardship or persecution or famine or nakedness or danger or sword?"

ROMANS 8:35, NIV

No, in all these things we are more than conquerors through him who loved us. For I am convinced that neither death nor life, neither angels nor demons, neither the present nor the future, nor any powers, neither height nor depth, nor anything else in all creation, will be able to separate us from the love of God that is in Christ Jesus our Lord.

ROMANS 8:37–39 (NIV)

"Let the peace of Christ rule in your hearts, since as members of one body you were called to peace. And be thankful"

COLOSSIANS 3:15, NIV

"Do not be anxious about anything, but in every situation, by prayer and petition, with thanksgiving, present your requests to God. And the peace of God, which transcends all understanding, will guard your hearts and your minds in Christ Jesus."

PHILIPPIANS 4:6–7, NIV

"I know what it is to be in need, and I know what it is to have plenty. I have learned the secret of being content in any and every situation, whether well fed or hungry, whether living in plenty or in want. I can do all this through him who gives me strength."

PHILIPPIANS 4:12–13, NIV

"Now to him who is able to do immeasurably more than all we ask or imagine, according to his power that is at work within us"

EPHESIANS 3:20, NIV

"Now may the Lord of peace himself give you peace at all times and in every way. The Lord be with all of you."

2 THESSALONIANS 3:16, NIV

"Let us then approach God's throne of grace with confidence, so that we may receive mercy and find grace to help us in our time of need."

HEBREWS 4:16, NIV

"Keep your lives free from the love of money and be content with what you have, because God has said, Never will I leave you; never will I forsake you." So we say with confidence, 'The Lord is my helper; I will not be afraid. What can mere mortals do to me?'"

HEBREWS 13:5–6, NIV

"Cast all your anxiety on him because he cares for you."

1 PETER 5:7, NKJV